C000224866

A PRACTICAL STEP-BY-STEP GUIDE

water gardens

A PRACTICAL STEP-BY-STEP GUIDE

water gardens

YVONNE REES ● NEIL SUTHERLAND   consultant: JENNY HENDY

PUBLISHED BY
SALAMANDER BOOKS LIMITED
LONDON

This edition published in 2001 by Salamander Books Ltd
8 Blenheim Court, Brewery Road,
London N7 9NY, United Kingdom

© 2001 Salamander Books Limited, London
A member of the Chrysalis Group plc

Some of the material that appears in this book was previously published in *A
Creative Step-by-Step Guide to the Water Garden*, also by Yvonne Rees.

ISBN 0-84065-319-1

Printed and bound in Spain

CREDITS

Series consultant: Jenny Hendy
Author of Plant Identifier section: Gwen Rigby
Designed and edited by: FOCUS PUBLISHING,
The Courtyard, 26 London Road, Sevenoaks, Kent TN13 1AP
Designers: Neil Adams, David Etherington
Editors: Guy Croton, Caroline Watson
Photographer: Neil Sutherland
Editorial director: Will Steeds
Production: Phillip Chamberlain

*Half-title page; frontispiece;
copyright page:*
All photographs by Neil Sutherland.

THE AUTHOR

Yvonne Rees has been involved with water gardening,
garden design and garden maintenance for over 20 years. She designs and
installs ponds and has written several books on water gardening, as well as
lecturing and broadcasting on the subject.

THE CONSULTANT

Jenny Hendy is a respected garden writer and author. With a lifelong
passion for gardening, she has been sharing her knowledge of planting and
design for the last fifteen years, through writing, lecturing and TV
appearances. She now also runs a successful garden design consultancy.

THE PHOTOGRAPHER

Neil Sutherland has more than 25 years' experience in a wide range of
photographic fields. His work has been published in countless books and
magazines.

CONTENTS

Left: Houttuynia cordata *'Plena'* has attractive heart-shaped, aromatic leaves and white spring flowers. It will thrive in shallow water or provide good ground cover in a damp, semi-shaded position.

THE BASICS

11

THE PLEASURES OF WATER GARDENING

A water feature in the garden is an instant focal point;
the gleam of a pond, the sparkle of a fountain or the fantastic shapes
and colours of lush water plants are irresistible.

Because water is so adaptable, any size, shape or style of garden can easily incorporate a stunning feature if you only have the confidence to include it in your plans, and if you take the time and trouble to plan it properly.

A large plot offers the chance to enjoy a good-sized pond, complete with a wide range of plants, a bog garden, maybe a bridge or stepping stones leading to an additional platform or island area. Smaller ponds for more moderate gardens can still offer a scaled-down range of exciting plants and moving water features, such as a fountain or a waterfall. Even a tiny patio or courtyard could be transformed by a wall-mounted water spout, a small bubble fountain or a pool or bog garden in a barrel.

As well as looking good, a water feature will attract a wide range of wildlife to your garden, not just frogs and toads, but also insects, such as dragonflies, different species of birds, and small mammals. A pool or cool, splashing fountain has a wonderful relaxing effect, too, converting your garden into an excellent retreat and an escape from the stress of everyday life.

Best of all, once it is installed and provided it is correctly constructed, a water feature is one of the easiest garden features to maintain. If installing one of these features is a little daunting, then this book will prove how simple and successful it can be, provided you only follow the instructions carefully. Then you will gain lasting pleasure from a special highlight of your garden.

Right: Aponogeton distachyos, *the water hawthorn.*

Right: *Lilies, iris and hostas.*

CHOOSING A POOL STYLE

A water feature in the garden can be so versatile that its size and style are limited only by your courage and imagination. If you do not find a preformed pool that inspires you, you can create virtually any kind of pool you please with the latest flexible liners.

Of course, when choosing a style of pool there are some practical issues to consider (see page 16), but this decision is crucial, for whatever its size and position, water is a natural focal point that will become a key feature in the garden the moment it is included; that flash of light reflecting the brightness and movement of the sky is guaranteed to capture the attention, and the wealth of interest a pool can offer is sure to hold it.

Once your pool has been installed, this is where you will want to spend most of your garden time, so make sure your new water feature is in keeping with the rest of your plants and features and really looks as though it 'belongs' in your garden. The smart terrace or patio, or the formally designed garden with its regular beds and borders, cries out for a suitably edged formal pool, either raised or sunken, in any manner of geometric shapes, from squares to rectangles and even circles and hexagons. Two or more formal pools can often be successfully linked, by interlocking similar shapes, or by arranging pools on different levels with the water spilling from one to another by means of a water pump. The informal pool, by comparison, should be a profusion of plants, a veritable jungle of lush moisture-lovers, such as marsh marigolds, astilbe, mimulus, reeds and rushes.

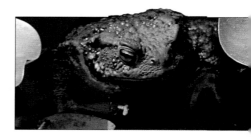

Above: *Even the smallest pond will soon offer a fascinating variety of wildlife for you to observe at your leisure. Frogs, toads and newts will be attracted to this new habitat.*

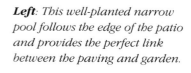

Left: *This well-planted narrow pool follows the edge of the patio and provides the perfect link between the paving and garden.*

Above: A bold approach often pays off. This large koi pool successfully dominates a modest-sized plot, featuring a timber-decked patio linked to the rest of the garden via a substantial bridge.

Below: A circular raised pool at the heart of the garden makes a perfectly integrated feature and can be enhanced by a small fountain to provide extra interest.

Below: A wildlife pond such as this might be comfortably integrated into the corner of a more formal garden and can be specifically designed to attract a wide range of birds, insects and small mammals.

Above: Lush planting with marginals and bog plants is the making of an informal pond.

CHOOSING A GOOD SITE

Once installed, a pool can be relatively trouble-free,
provided you position and build it correctly.

Although there are few locations where a pool is completely impractical, if you want to grow a few plants and maintain a healthy ecological balance in the water, you are advised to choose an open, sunny site away from any deciduous trees whose falling leaves can make such a mess of the water in the autumn, ruining the effect of the feature.

*This pool is sited
too close to the tree.*

Above: *Avoid proximity
to trees wherever possible.
As well as casting shade,
deciduous trees create a
problem with leaves that decay
and pollute the water when
they fall into the pond.*

Left: *For a pool to look good
and in keeping with its
surroundings, ensure that its
shape and position fit the overall
plan of your garden and that
plants and construction
materials are linked visually
to nearby features.*

Consider, too, when planning a sunken pool, that there may be problems under the ground, such as old foundations, gas or water pipes, power cables or drains. (Apart from anything else, you need to proceed carefully if you are doing any deep digging). If re-siting any of these is too expensive, or a sunken pool is just not practical, then you may have to consider a raised pool.

Sometimes the ideal site for a pool suggests itself: within the design of a patio, for example, or where there is a natural damp depression in the ground. Often a pool can be worked into the existing contours of the garden, into one corner, or set parallel with the straight edges of a paved area or patio. It makes sense to choose a site as close to the house as possible. This not only gives you instant access to the poolside, but also means that you can see and enjoy the pond from the comfort of your home in bad weather; it will be closer to a power source for running pumps and lighting, too. You can also create wonderful reflections of your house lit up at night in the water surface.

Another important consideration if you have a young family is that pools and ponds must be positioned where they can be safely fenced off so that children can't fall in.

If you find it difficult to imagine the size and shape of the finished pool in the context of your garden, try drawing up a scaled diagram, then use pegs and string to mark out the shape on the ground.

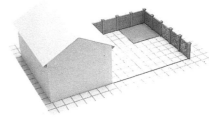

Above: *Siting the pool too close to the fence creates construction and maintenance problems.*

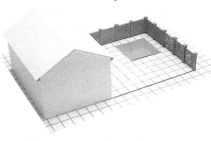

Above: *Moving the pool away from the corner gives you access to the area behind it. Landscape this with a rockery or a bold planting scheme.*

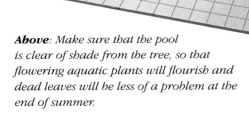

Above: *Make sure that the pool is clear of shade from the tree, so that flowering aquatic plants will flourish and dead leaves will be less of a problem at the end of summer.*

Right: *A pool near the house not only means easy access in all weathers, but also makes the feature an attractive focal point that you can view from indoors.*

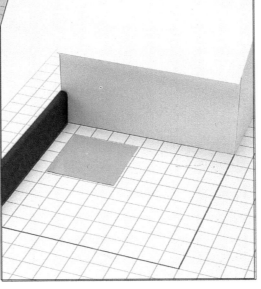

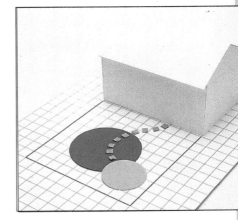

Above: *If the pool is at the other end of the garden, provide some kind of safe, dry access from the house in wet weather via a path or stepping stones.*

LINING OPTIONS

The choice of liner comes down to your budget, the location – whether the pool is going to be at ground level or raised – and whether you are going to insist on creative control over the shape of the pool or are happy to go with a preformed one.

Unless you are paying a professional to design and/or excavate your pool, waterproofing it with some kind of lining material is almost certainly going to be your greatest expense. There are no really cheap options: the less expensive materials will still take a fair slice of your budget, and even then they will not perform as well as those at the top of the range. Compromising on size and style is the only way you can reasonably cut costs. Another very important point to bear in mind before you buy is that the more accurate your measurements, the less wastage there is, so do double check all your calculations. (Some people still favour concrete for lining a pool, but be aware that concreting a pool is not a job for a novice).

The easiest type of liners to buy are the preformed pools, which are available in

Above: This informal pool has been made with a rigid plastic liner. The pebble edging planted with creeping ground cover protects the pool from grass clippings.

Left: This rigid plastic shell is typical of a wide range of preformed shapes you can buy to enable you to create an 'instant' pond in your garden.

Once installed, you can disguise the rim with an edging of your choice.

Most rigid pool have a shelf at the right depth to support pots of marginal plants.

A depth of at least 60cm (24in) here will enable fish to overwinter in ice-free water.

A SELECTION OF LINING MATERIALS

PVC (polyvinyl chloride) liner 0.5mm(0.02in) thick for smaller pools only.

Inexpensive polythene material in black, blue, brown and green.

LDPE (low-density polyethylene) liner 0.5mm(0.02in) thick.

EPDM (ethylene propylene diene rubber membrane) 1mm(0.04in) thick. Very durable.

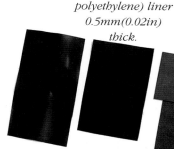

These are non-woven polyester underlays for cushioning the liner.

PVC blend with a high plasticiser content to improve flexibility and durability. Also 0.5mm(0.02in) thick.

Butyl (isobutylene isoprene rubber) 0.75mm(0.03in) thick. Very strong and long lasting.

a choice of sizes and shapes, including both formal and informal styles. Most incorporate a marginal shelf for plants. The cheapest of these are made of thin plastic and are fairly flimsy so do need to be handled and installed carefully. Their durability is fairly limited, too. Rigid pools are also available in much thicker plastic and these should last for many years. Much stronger but more expensive are the preformed GRP (glass reinforced plastic) shapes, which can be bought in an equally wide variety of styles to suit every garden.

The most popular type of liner is the flexible type: you buy it in a piece, or off a roll, and it stretches to fit every contour of your excavation. Inexpensive PVC (polyvinyl chloride) and polythene liners can be prone to fading or splitting after a few years of exposure to sunlight and cold winters. Several other types of plastic are sold for pools and these are often guaranteed for up to 20 years. If you intend your feature to be permanent, you may wish to choose a butyl rubber liner, a highly durable material available in various thicknesses.

RAISED POOLS

The big advantage of a raised pool is that there is no digging and relatively little disturbance to the garden or patio. You can easily integrate a raised pool with other features, such as seating and raised beds. There may be practical reasons why a raised pool is preferable: a difficult site with bedrock just below the surface; a high water table; a sloping garden or simply a small budget. If you want to make a raised pool using a liner or a preformed unit, it is best to choose a circular or oval shape to help the pool withstand the pressure of the water; without the support of soil around it, a square-edged design would be prone to splitting or breaking down at the corners.

***Above**: A formal raised pool with a fountain makes an excellent focal point to the patio, drive or lawn.*

On a formal patio, you can edge the pool with pavers or brick to match the patio, and remember that the wide rim of coping stones makes a handy place to sit and watch the water or to stand pots of suitable plants.

PREPARING A LINER POOL

Preparation is the key to creating a successful pool. Don't rush the way you remove the turf, don't stop digging until you have exactly the contour you want, even though it will involve hard physical labour, and position the liner carefully.

Mark out the shape of your proposed pool on the grass or soil using a hosepipe or pegs and string. This allows you to walk round the area and view it from every angle – even from above if you can see from a nearby window – and to adjust the outline until you are satisfied it looks right. Cut turfs from the area using a sharp-edged spade, lift and roll them root side out, and keep them damp until you need them around the pool or elsewhere in the garden. Next, remove the topsoil, taking care not to mix it with any subsoil or rubble, and also put it to one side for further use. You can now begin the serious digging of the subsoil. If you have not planned to use it to contour the area around the pool or to create other raised features, arrange for the waste to be taken away. Dig out the subsoil to your required depth – a minimum of 60cm (24in) and usually no more than about

Right: *The edge of the flexible liner is just visible at the back margin of this small informal pool. Being black helps it to blend in with the water surface.*

Use gloves when handling this – the fibres can irritate skin.

1 *To protect the liner against damage, use a custom-made pond cushioning material or use a layer of sand, old carpet, sacking or loft insulation material, as here. It is vital that the liner is afforded at least some protection.*

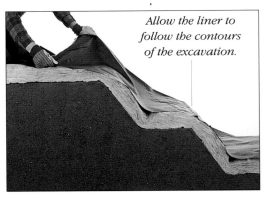

Allow the liner to follow the contours of the excavation.

2 *Lay the pool liner over the excavated hole, taking care that there is an equal amount of excess around the outside. For large pools, you will need help moving the liner, as it can become very heavy and unwieldy.*

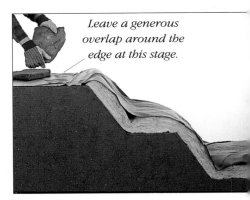

Leave a generous overlap around the edge at this stage.

3 *Anchor the edges of the liner down with smooth slabs, boulders or bricks. You can move these around as the pool fills with water to help the liner settle into place.*

120cm (48in). Remember to incorporate a shelf for marginal plants about 25cm (10in) below the final water level. About 30cm (12in) wide should be sufficient for positioning plant baskets. Most importantly, you must make sure your excavations are completely level; if the sides vary in height, the pool will look very strange once it is filled with water. The easiest way to achieve this is to knock a 120cm (48in) post into the centre of your pool area. Use this to balance one end of a straight edge extended from a series of small 30cm (12in) pegs or posts sited around the edge of the bank. Place a spirit level along the top to show you where any adjustments need to be made to ensure a level finish. When the excavations are complete and the sides are level, go over the base and sides by hand for a final check, making sure there are no major bumps or hollows, and remove any sharp stones that might damage your liner.

The maximum depth of water in the middle of the pool is 60cm (24in).

This marginal shelf is 30cm (12in) wide with about 25cm (10in) of water above it.

Above: *This profile represents a small liner pool once it has been filled for the first time. This setup is used on the following pages to show edging options and how to install pumps.*

Keep adjusting the material around the outside and tuck in any folds.

Adding water slowly enables you to stay in control as the liner settles.

4 *Now fill the pool slowly using a hosepipe to produce a steady trickle of water. The weight of the water will pull the liner into place.*

5 *When the pool has filled to its level, cut away any excess, leaving about 30cm (12in) to be anchored and hidden by your choice of edging.*

HOW MUCH LINER?

Add twice the maximum depth of the pool to both the overall length and width. Thus, a pool 3 x 1.8 x 0.6m deep (10ft x 6ft x 2ft) needs a liner 4.2 x 3m (14 x 10ft). Liner is flexible and stretches to fit with the weight of the water, so there is no need to allow for the gentle contouring of an informal pool or the extra few inches of a marginal shelf.

NATURAL EDGES

The way you finish off the edge of your pond is vital to the impression you create. The more natural-looking options extend from relaying the turf so that the pool cunningly blends back into the landscape, to surrounding the pool with sympathetic materials such as large stone slabs or wooden decking.

Marginal and moisture-loving plants do an excellent job of disguising and softening the edge of ponds, especially where you want to achieve a natural informal look. But you cannot plant them all the way round; you need access to the water, maybe even a place to sit near the water's edge, where you can relax and observe plants and wildlife at close quarters.

Grassy banks are perfect for informal ponds and streams, being complementary to both plants and other natural materials, such as stone and timber. You could even use it in a formal way where a geometrically shaped pool is set into a lawn.

The grass can be inset with other elements, such as bricks or pavers for a formal look or random stone or slabs for a more natural style. A wide flat stone close by the water's edge makes a useful seat or hard standing for a plant container, ornament or sculpture. Alternatively, add areas of other natural materials, such as a cluster of boulders interspersed with plants; well-weathered timber or railway sleepers sunk into the grass; perhaps a small beach of pebbles running down into the water.

If you do not have the time and patience to sow seed and wait for the grass to grow, turves create the perfect instant effect. Ideally, you should use the turves saved from your pool excavation, provided you lifted and rolled them carefully. You can also buy them commercially. Buy good-quality turves and be sure to keep them well watered until you are ready to use them.

Above: A turf edging instantly gives a completely natural look to a pool and is easy to lay. The pool liner can be tucked beneath the soil and turves to keep it firmly anchored.

Use slabs that will not become too slippery if they get wet.

Above: Grass with random stone slabs is one of the most attractive options for an informal pool. The slabs can be set on sand at intervals around the edge, slightly overlapping the water to help hide and anchor the lining material.

TIMBER DECKING

Timber decking can be a quick and inexpensive alternative for pool edging. Whether raised well away from the water or close to it, it looks extremely stylish, yet is relatively easy to construct and flexible enough to create a wide range of effects. It can also be extremely useful for solving practical problems such as levelling a sloping or uneven site where building a retaining wall and backfilling would make a paved patio too expensive. Decking is also useful for linking features together, or converting a raised pool into a sunken one. The timber most commonly used for decking is a good water-repellent hardwood such as teak or oak, or one of the less expensive African hardwoods. This will require a couple of coats of preservative after installation, then an extra coat every spring or autumn.

Above: Timber decking is an excellent and stylish companion for large pools, where it can be used to create simple platform areas, jetties, bridges and walkways. By overhanging the water, a deck not only provides the opportunity to observe fish and plants at close quarters, but also makes the pool look larger than it really is. Timber decking combines well with other materials and because it can be built to any size and shape, the design possibilities are endless.

Use a wood preservative that will not harm pond life.

Right: Unless you want to create a natural sloping beach effect running into the pool, an edging of pebbles or small stones needs to be contained by wooden battens to prevent the stones spilling into the water. Use only washed stone to reduce the risk of introducing dirt or debris into the pool.

Use the larger grade of chips rather than the finer composted type.

Right: Bark chips can make an attractive edging alternative in an informal garden or woodland-type setting. Again, a wooden batten is useful to prevent the chips floating off into the water.

23

EDGING WITH SLABS AND BRICKS

For a formal look you can't beat the regular shapes of bricks or dressed or manufactured stone, while for a semi-formal look try broken flagstones with attractive plants in the gaps between them.

Unit paving – that is, bricks, slabs, stone setts and stones, as opposed to continuous, poured concrete – is perfect for all but the most informal pool. It provides a neat and attractive finish that remains dry and practical underfoot, and which can be satisfactorily coordinated with, or matched to, other garden features. It easily disguises the pool edges and is perfect for weighting down or hiding those liner edges. Even better, it offers an infinite variety of creative possibilities, from

Below: This random arrangement of broken flagstones not only conceals the liner but also creates a delightfully informal, yet practical, hard surface around this small garden pool.

The lawn edge here echoes the informal style of the pool and provides a smooth transition to the rest of the garden.

mixing materials to laying them in unusual patterns, or even growing creeping plants in the cracks between them. You can use just a few slabs as a pool edging or extend the plan to create a full-scale patio or seating and eating area. Bricks and pavers come in a wide variety of colours, finishes, shapes and sizes, and some are designed to interlock and create sophisticated designs. Make sure that your chosen paving is frost and rain proof. Bricks are prone to splitting or flaking, so only use good-quality paving bricks. Thorough preparation of the ground is also essential for success. The foundations must be stable, not damp and boggy – even good friable soil is too crumbly. Rocky hardcore is far better and this can be used to backfill wherever you have had to excavate unsuitable soil. Remember that the finished level is crucial, so measure the depth of layers carefully.

Above: A brick border around a circular pool is quite tricky to install, but with patience the results can be stunning, as in this semi-formal pool.

A brick edging needs good foundations: a 15cm(6in) layer of hardcore, 2.5cm(1in) of sand and 2.5cm(1in) of cement. By overlapping the edge of the pool slightly, the liner is completely concealed for a neat finish.

The bricks slope slightly away from the water to prevent run-off into the pool.

Cement
Sand
Hardcore

Paving slabs have a larger surface area to spread the weight of the people walking on them. They need only a 7.5cm (3in) layer of hardcore to give some substance to a damp or too crumbly soil base.

Check that slabs are level at every stage using a spirit level. Make sure that the total paved area slopes slightly backwards away from the water.

Cement
Sand
Hardcore

A PEBBLE BEACH

Pebbles make for an unusual edge or edge feature, but make sure the pebbles or stones have no sharp edges that might pierce the liner, and wash them first to avoid introducing any unwanted debris or chemicals into the pool.

A pebble beach makes an attractive informal edge for a natural effect pond or an oriental-style pool, and is also a good choice if you are planning a wildlife water garden, as birds and small mammals need a sloping edge to approach the water safely. Smooth pebbles here will protect the liner from damage and maintain an attractive appearance. A grassy bank would quickly become a muddy quagmire under the onslaught of tiny feet. The pebbles must be smooth to prevent them damaging the liner and these are available graded into different sizes. When you excavate the pool, gently shape one side or a small area into a sloping bank – there is no need to install a beach all the way round the pool. Visually, an area of bank looks more attractive and provides the opportunity to incorporate a marginal shelf for growing an interesting range of water-loving plants. When you calculate your liner, allow extra width so that you can run it a good way up the slope. Anchor the end of the liner with soil, slabs or boulders, depending on the effect you are aiming for. Try to link the pebbles to the immediate surrounding area, either by running them up to a small bog garden for a totally natural effect or by inserting pebble sections into a paved area in a more formal design. Run the pebbles right down into the water for the most natural look.

Left: A carefully constructed pebble edging blends the formal with the informal in this charming patio pool with its millstone fountain.

Left: Pebbles are ideally suited to an informal area, the banks softened by striking marginal plants. When positioning heavy stones, place on folded pond liner to cushion the weight.

Below: An area of rough stones is the perfect maintenance-free setting for a novel poolside sculpture, and fully complements both the water and the lush planting scheme around it.

Above: Pebbled shallows create their own small feature area at the corner of a much larger pool. You can buy a wide range of pebbles, cobbles and boulders in various sizes and colours. Wash them thoroughly before use.

AQUATIC BASKETS, LINERS AND SOIL

Containers need to be right for the size of plant and the shape of the pool, and the soil has to be of a type suitable for pool planting.

Water plants can be planted directly into the soil or mulch at the bottom of the pool or on the marginal shelf, and with a large natural pool or lake this is often the most practical option. However, with smaller pools, using special rot-proof plastic pots and containers makes the plants – and pond – much easier to handle.

A wide range of containers is available, their sides perforated to keep the soil moist and aerated. Baskets tend to have a wide base to make them stable and are usually black, which makes them virtually invisible once they are in the water. Large-weave baskets need lining with hessian or woven plastic material to prevent the soil washing away, but the containers with a close-weave pattern do not need lining.

The soil you use for aquatic plants should be a rich and heavy loam to ensure that it has plenty of nutrients and remains waterlogged. A clay soil has the right consistency, but is usually not rich enough; sandy or chalky soils are too fine and will wash out of the containers. Make sure that any soil you use is free from chemicals or herbicides.

This large plastic bowl is ideal for the more vigorous water lilies.

Hessian lining material

This type of planting basket is fine for water lilies in the early stages. Tiny perforations eliminate the need for a hessian liner.

Louvred sides prevent the loss of soil into the water.

Most water lilies can be planted in low-sided plastic bowls such as this.

A sturdy plastic bowl is ideal for small and miniature water lilies.

Glyceria spectabilis 'Variegata', an attractively striped grass that grows about 60cm(24in) high.

Hydrocotyle vulgaris, a low-growing marginal that produces delicate nodding blooms.

The marsh marigold, Caltha palustris, a popular and dependable marginal plant.

These marginal baskets are designed to take a selection of plants and are curved to fit the edge of a circular or other informal shape of pool.

AQUATIC SOIL

You can buy special potting mixtures recommended for water plants from garden centres and aquatic specialists. Avoid general garden potting mixtures, as these contain peat (too acidic for most aquatic plants) and soluble fertilisers. Only use special water plant fertiliser and never manure, which can encourage the growth of algae.

Large-weave plastic container for lilies and marginals

Square fine-meshed basket for large marginals

Circular baskets with louvred sides and fine perforations are ideal for lilies and larger marginal plants. They do not need lining.

Plastic liner for large mesh containers

Water-retaining potting mixture formulated for aquatic plants.

Small stones, pebbles or gravel as a top dressing to retain soil in containers.

Mimulus luteus 'Nana', an attractive marginal plant.

A small planting pot with fine mesh panels.

SETTING UP A WATER PUMP

A fountain is one of the first pool features people add, not just for the attractive look and sound, but also because it helps to aerate the water.

If you have sufficient depth of water, a submersible pump is a neat way to run some kind of moving water feature, such as a fountain or waterfall. The pump remains submerged below the water level, making it easier to keep both the pump and pipework concealed. Submersibles are also easier to maintain and more economical to run than surface-mounted pumps.

It is very important to calculate the size of pump you need accurately or the results may be very disappointing, especially if you are hoping to run more than one feature from

You can connect this foam filter directly to the pump or at the end of a plastic tube.

Extension tube

Geyser fountain head

Bell fountain head

These adapters allow you to connect tubing of various diameters.

This part of the pump casing houses a block of plastic filter foam.

This is the electric motor that drives a spinning impeller to draw in water.

This T-piece allows you to divert water into two outlets.

Water flow control

Use this cap to blank off the outlet.

This fountain head produces a three-tier spray of jets.

This head produces two tiers of higher jets.

These are two samples of clear plastic tubing that will fit this pump. Black tubing is also sold for water pumps.

Internal diameter of 19mm(0.75in).

Internal diameter of 25mm(1in).

the same pump using a T-piece in the outlet pipe. As the head of water increases, so the output will decrease; the length of pipe, its bore and the number of bends will also affect performance. It is not a good idea to run your pump at full capacity all the time, so it is better to buy a model slightly larger than your needs.

Installing the pump is simple enough, provided it is close to a convenient outdoor electrical point. This supply should only be installed by a qualified electrician.

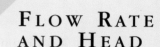
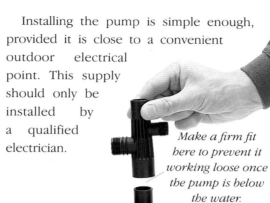

Make a firm fit here to prevent it working loose once the pump is below the water.

1 *If you want to use the built-in filter simply push it over the inlet pipe of the pump until it clicks into place. It is easy to remove for cleaning.*

2 *If you plan to run a fountain and perhaps a waterfall as well, push the T-piece adapter onto the outlet pipe of the pump.*

FLOW RATE AND HEAD

When you start to look for a suitable water pump for your pool you will see that the specifications mention flow rate per hour and maximum head of water. Bear in mind that the widest bore tubing that you can fit to the pump will help you achieve the optimum flow rate. 'Head' also reflects the power of the pump but in terms of the height the water can be pumped to in relation to the water level in the pool. Often, the flow rate is quoted at various heads.

3 *Screw on this blanking cap if you decide not to run a waterfall from the adaptor. You can easily change your mind and fit a tube instead.*

4 *Set up like this, the pump is ready to have a fountain head fitted on top of the outlet pipe. The built-in foam pad will filter the water as it is sucked through the vents in the casing.*

The water will flow up this pipe.

With this outlet blanked off, all the water will flow upwards.

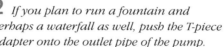

You need to fit this adjusting screw whatever outlets you plan to supply. As you screw it further in, the projection obstructs the upward water flow.

INSTALLING A FOUNTAIN

The splash and glitter of a fountain or water jet add
excitement and pleasure to the smallest pool.

Once you have put in the pump, installing a fountain could not be simpler; all you need is a fountain nozzle or jet, a length of plastic tubing and jubilee clips to connect them. Nozzles and jets come in a wide choice of types producing different effects, from tall plumes and multiple spray sequences, to a small bell or dome which is suitable for smaller pools. The mechanism might be hidden by an ornamental device, such as a human figure, a dolphin or other animal; or be skilfully incorporated into a classical or abstract sculpture. Some fountains come complete with lights and even music choreographed to the spray sequence. If you only have a tiny patio, or you have young children, you might prefer the option of a concealed reservoir where the water is recycled through a wall spout (via an old tap, a lion's head, a sculpted face or whatever you choose) into a small basin; or alternatively you could allow it to bubble over a bed of pebbles. There is something to suit everyone's taste, and style and size of garden.

*For best results, position the spray
fountain head just above water level.*

*Control the height of the fountain by
adjusting this water flow regulator.*

*Raise the pump on bricks to bring the
fountain head to the correct level. This
also helps to prevent the pump sucking
in debris at the bottom of the pool.*

Left: *This is the simplest way to provide a
fountain. The submersible pump draws in water
and forces it through the fountain head.*

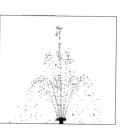

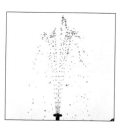

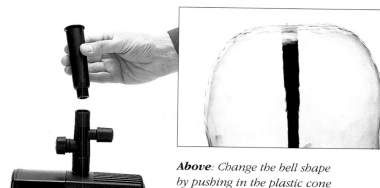

Above: *The fountain head with three circles of holes produces a three-tier pattern with a wide spread of water. Make sure the pool is large enough to catch the spray.*

Above: *The fountain head with two circles of holes produces a taller, two-tier pattern of water droplets.*

Above: *Change the bell shape by pushing in the plastic cone at the top of the head. Start with a reduced water flow and gradually increase it until the bell is the size you want.*

1 Once you have fitted the T-piece into the top outlet of the pump, simply select the type of fountain head you wish to use. Most pumps are supplied with a choice of two spray patterns.

2 For a change from the spray pattern, try a bell fountain head. Correctly adjusted, this produces a smooth and symmetrical dome of water.

Air drawn in through these holes creates a frothy flow of water.

Push the geyser head firmly onto the extension tube. You can alter the angle of the head to create different water flow patterns.

3 For a geyser fountain, first fit the extension tube onto the T-piece. This will raise the head well above the water level.

Above: *The geyser fountain head produces a strong jet of aerated water. To get the best effect with this head, operate the pump at its most powerful setting.*

INSTALLING A WATER FILTER

Filtering the water in your pool not only makes a healthier environment for any planting you have done, but is an essential consideration if you also have fish in your pond.

A healthy pond relies on the correct biological balance between plants and animal life to keep unwelcome toxins and algae build-up to a minimum. In a large natural pool nature makes its own adjustments and, provided you keep rampant plants in check, you should not have any problems with green scummy water or waste materials from fish. However, in smaller pools with synthetic linings you may need to install a water filter. This will circulate the water and keep it well-aerated and is a practical and economic consideration for small ponds. There are two main types of filter: you can recycle the water through an external system, which can be run off an existing pump, or you can install a sump at the bottom of the pool that filters the water through sand and stones or gravel via a separate pump. This usually incorporates a gauze filter pad that can be removed for cleaning. The simple filter system featured here will strain out particles of debris and suspended algae and will also reduce the levels of toxic wastes.

Above: Goldfish are hardy and tolerant of a wide range of water conditions, but a biological filter will help to keep the pond clean and clear.

1 *With the side cut away you can see how the pipework is arranged inside this typical biological filter suitable for small ponds up to 2,300 litres (600 gallons) in capacity.*

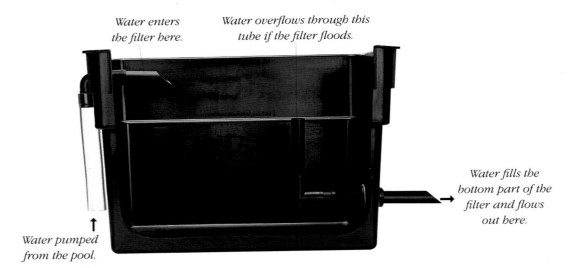

Water enters the filter here.

Water overflows through this tube if the filter floods.

Water fills the bottom part of the filter and flows out here.

Water pumped from the pool.

These provide a large surface area for beneficial bacteria to colonise.

2 *The bottom of the tank is filled with a biological filter medium. Here this consists of plastic corrugated pipe sections. These are inert and do not affect the water chemistry.*

The top layer of foam is a coarser grade than the lower one.

3 *Two layers of plastic foam cover the filter medium. These strain out any debris in the water flowing from the pond. This layer allows easy filter maintenance.*

4 *The filter is now ready for use. Make sure that the coarse grade of foam forms the top layer. Place the filter on a firm, level surface. Make sure that the filter unit is well camouflaged by rocks and plants by planning for it in advance.*

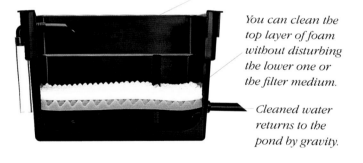

In use a lid covers the top.

You can clean the top layer of foam without disturbing the lower one or the filter medium.

Cleaned water returns to the pond by gravity.

Run the filter at reduced water flow at first to allow colonies of aerobic bacteria to build up on the filter medium.

Right: *Here a submersible pump powers a spray fountain and a biological filter at the side of the pond. Place the filter above the pond water level so that the cleaned water flows back freely under gravity.*

HOW A BIOFILTER CLEANS THE WATER

A biological filter is so-called because it uses the biological processes of naturally occurring bacteria to clean the water of harmful biochemicals. The streams, rivers, lakes and seas of the world abound in bacteria. Some need oxygen to flourish and are therefore called aerobic bacteria. Among these are two groups that break down animal wastes into less harmful substances. The first group go to work on the highly toxic ammonia that animals excrete. They break this down to nitrites. Unfortunately, nitrites are also dangerously poisonous to most water creatures, even in low concentrations. Thankfully, the second group of aerobic bacteria break nitrites down to nitrates, which are much less toxic and are absorbed by plants as food.

35

OXYGENATING PLANTS

A selection of oxygenating plants is essential for the good health of your pool, especially if the pond is new.

Oxygenators are mostly submerged, or occasionally floating, species of water plants that use up waste nutrients in the water by means of their underwater foliage. This, and the fact that such plants grow prolifically, will quickly deprive bothersome algae of nutrients and minerals, and thus help to keep the water clean.

This group of plants is not particularly attractive; in fact, few oxygenators are as noticeably pretty as the water violet, *Hottonia palustris*, which produces a mass of pale mauve flowers above a dense

underwater mat of fern-like foliage, but they generally do their job well, not only preventing green water and blanketweed, but also providing useful cover for pond insects and small fish.

For the average pool, you will need about five clumps per m² (one oxygenating plant for every 2ft²) of surface area. Larger pools, over 14m² (150ft²) can reduce that requirement to nearer three bunches per m² (one plant per 3ft²).

Different species flourish at different times of year, so you will need a selection of at least two or three species.

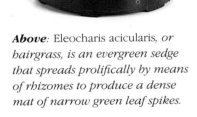

Above: Eleocharis acicularis, *or hairgrass, is an evergreen sedge that spreads prolifically by means of rhizomes to produce a dense mat of narrow green leaf spikes.*

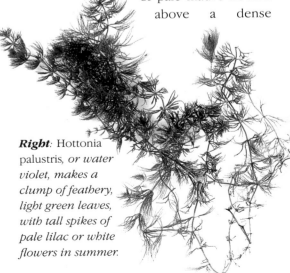

Right: Hottonia palustris, *or water violet, makes a clump of feathery, light green leaves, with tall spikes of pale lilac or white flowers in summer.*

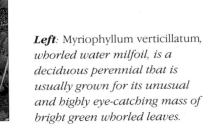

Left: Myriophyllum verticillatum, *whorled water milfoil, is a deciduous perennial that is usually grown for its unusual and highly eye-catching mass of bright green whorled leaves.*

OXYGENATORS

*Callitriche hermaphroditica
   (C. autumnalis)*
Callitriche palustris (C. verna)
Ceratophyllum demersum
Crassula recurva
Eleocharis acicularis
Fontinalis antipyretica
Hottonia palustris
*Lagarosiphon major
   (Elodea crispa)*
Myriophyllum proserpinacoides
Myriophyllum verticillatum
Potamogeton crispus
Ranunculus aquatilis

Above: Lagarosiphon major *is a perennial oxygenator that will spread into a dark green blanket of attractively curled feathery stems.*

Above: *The tiny, semi-evergreen leaves of* Lagarosiphon major *(also known as* Elodea crispa*) are clustered along each stem.*

Right: *Hardy* Ceratophyllum demersum, *or hornwort, grows best in cool water, where it spreads to make a submerged mat of tiny dark green leaves.*

Below: Ranunculus aquatilis, *the water buttercup, has bright green feathery foliage that can be invasive if not kept in check.*

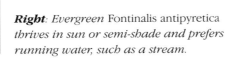

Right: *Evergreen* Fontinalis antipyretica *thrives in sun or semi-shade and prefers running water, such as a stream.*

FLOATING PLANTS

These plants are an essential part of the flora of your pool, include a number of oxygenators, are easy to plant (you just launch them on the water) and help restrict the amount of sunlight getting into the pond – although you need to make sure some species don't take over the pool.

Floating plants are all those that are unrooted – that is, they float on, or just below, the surface of the water. Most of them require a water depth of about 30–90cm (12–36in) and are generally very easy to install, simply by resting the plant gently on the water surface and allowing it to find its own level. Naturally, this group includes a large number of oxygenators and, like oxygenators (see pages 36–37), floating plants will grow quickly within a single season. Consequently, you may need to take them out of the water to cut them back before they become too rampant.

Floating plants, such as the sturdy and beautiful water hyacinth (*Eichhornia crassipes*) or the tiny-leaved frogbit (*Hydrocharis morsus-ranae*) not only look good but also, unlike water lilies, grow quickly and establish useful cover within months of being put into the water. For this reason, it is not generally recommended that you put prolific floating plants into very large ponds. Unless you can devise some means of removing them, such plants could quickly become a pest and dominate the entire feature.

A SELECTION OF FLOATING PLANTS

Azolla filiculoides (Fairy moss)
Eichhornia crassipes
    (Water hyacinth)
Hydrocharis morsus-ranae
    (Frogbit)
Lemna trisulca
    (Ivy-leaved duckweed)
Pistia stratiotes (Water lettuce)
Riccia fluitans (Crystalwort)
Stratiotes aloides (Water soldier)
Trapa natans (Water chestnut)
Utricularia vulgaris (Bladderwort)

Left: *The floating annual,* Trapa natans, *or water chestnut, is grown for its attractive triangular leaves, white summer flowers and edible nuts.*

Left: *Provide tropical or subtropical conditions for the short-lived, tender perennial water lettuce, Pistia stratiotes. Fresh green leaves grow from the centre.*

Below: *The water hyacinth, Eichhornia crassipes, is a glossy evergreen or semi-evergreen water plant with attractive round-edged leaves.*

Above: *Once it is established, perennial water hyacinth, Eichhornia crassipes, produces beautiful lilac flower spikes each summer.*

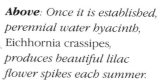

Supported by air-filled leaf stalks, this plant can become invasive in warm conditions.

Above: *The ivy-leaved, or star duckweed, Lemna trisulca, makes a mat of tiny green fronds, which are excellent for purifying the water.*

Above: Azolla filiculoides *comes from a family of floating water ferns that help to control pond algae. Reduce it using a net if it spreads too much.*

Right: *The hardy water soldier Stratiotes aloides, likes limestone waters and plenty of sun. In these conditions, it produces tiny white flowers in summer.*

Right: *Planting a water soldier is simply a matter of placing it in the water. It remains mostly submerged but rises to the surface in summer.*

MARGINAL PLANTS (1)

The plants that grow naturally along the banks and shallows of ponds and streams are among the most dramatic and beautiful species you could wish to feature in your garden.

As a group, marginal plants include a wonderful variety of size, shape and colour within the range of their foliage alone, while some have spectacular flowers, too, at certain times of the year. Even if your water feature is small, you will surely have space for one or two of these eye-catching plants, if only to feature as a focal point within your garden scheme. Marginal plants are widely available from garden and aquatic centres. Always choose young, healthy specimens.

These plants are usually positioned on the marginal shelf, specially built just below the surface of the water, so that these mud-loving plants can keep their roots waterlogged. You can plant them directly onto the shelf in soil enriched with humus or pot them up into specially perforated plastic baskets for easy maintenance.

Right: Iris laevigata *will flourish in the shallows or in the moist soil of a bog garden or pool edge. The blooms appear above the spreading clump of smooth, green, spearlike leaves in early to mid-summer. Varieties of* Iris laevigata *include 'Regale', which has red blooms, and 'Snowdrift', which is white. 'Atropurpurea' has purple flowers.*

40

Iris pseudacorus *'Variegata'*. *The flowers appear from early to mid-summer.*

Iris ensata (I. kaempferi) *'Variegata'*

Above: *Pontedaria cordata, or pickerel weed, is popular as a marginal plant both for its pretty blue-mauve flower spikes and its lush, glossy green leaves.*

Scirpus albescens

Ranunculus flammula

Cotula coronopifolia *'Brass Buttons'*

Myriophyllum proserpinacoides *(Also featured as an oxygenator)*

41

MARGINAL PLANTS (2)

However attracted you are to the idea of marginal plants, don't go mad. Buy a few and
see how they settle in and expand, and then start thinking about adding
a few more to fill in any gaps.

Marginal plants can add so much to the final appearance of your pond or pool. Apart from making a bit of a show, marginal plants help to soften the edges of a pool or stream; they might hide the liner and take away the rawness of a new excavation. Or the more dramatic species could add height and interest to an otherwise uninteresting garden. It is not a good idea to plant marginals all the way around the pool on the shelf provided, as this would totally obscure the pool itself and deny you access to the water's edge. It is more usual to plant up about one-third of the circumference as a kind of backdrop and gradually add more plants where you feel they might be needed. If they are positioned correctly, marginal plants not only provide visual interest but also give some shelter from prevailing winds and can be used to shade part of the water from midday sunshine. Minute forms of pondlife also enjoy the habitat created by the stems and roots submerged in the mud just below the water surface. Even young plants will lend an air of instant maturity and, in the rich, waterlogged soil, grow quickly to make it look as though the feature had always been there.

Above*: A dense growth of water forget-me-not,* Myosotis scorpioides (M. palustris), *brings summer colour to the pond edge. This delightful plant will thrive in shallow water as a marginal or in moist soil as a bog plant.*

Mentha aquatica

Juncus effusus
spiralis

Right: Juncus effusus, the soft rush, is one of the prettiest rushes. In summer, the mass of slender green stems is dotted with brown flower panicles.

Above: *In spring, the yellow skunk cabbage,* Lysichiton americanus, *is a striking sight alongside streams or pond. The shiny yellow arum-like flowers appear before the huge banana-shaped leaves, and give off a strange scent.*

Iris laevigata 'Variegata'

Myosotis scorpioides 'Mermaid'

Lysichiton camtschatcensis. *(This and* L. americanus *will also flourish as bog plants in moist soil.)*

Mimulus guttatus

43

MARGINAL PLANTS (3)

There is so much variety among water-loving plants that all the normal considerations of shape and colour in your planting scheme have to be dealt with.

Even if yours is a modestly sized pond and you only need a few plants, you can have fun planning your marginal plants. The wide range of plant sizes and shapes offers the chance to contrast spiky reed and sword shapes with large shiny discs, delicate hearts, feathery ferns and fluttering plumes. There is a huge range of colours among the foliage of

Above: Houttuynia cordata 'Plena' has attractive heart-shaped, aromatic leaves and white spring flowers. It will thrive in shallow water or provide good ground cover in a damp semi-shaded position.

Houttuynia cordata 'Plena'

Typha latifolia 'Variegata'

Preslia cervina (American water mint)

Sisyrinchium 'Boreale'

Zantedeschia aethiopica

Houttuynia cordata 'Chameleon'

marginal plants, too: greys, greens, yellow, gold and silver can be coordinated and contrasted to make the perfect blend of form and hue. Flowers can be used for seasonal interest or to create a sudden burst of colour as a focal point, and because they have an instant lush appeal, such plants can cunningly create the impression of water even if the pond or stream is 'dry'. Within an informal water garden you can achieve an interesting yet pleasant harmony; around the formal pool, the dramatic shapes and forms of marginal plants used in small groups have the perfect architectural impact.

Right: Golden club (Orontium aquaticum) *produces these distinctive yellow flowers on pure white stems during spring. The robust leaves stand out of the water or lie on the surface. Golden club will thrive in deeper water and can be lowered off the marginal shelf further out into the pond once established.*

Ranunculus grandiflora

Eleocharis palustris

Veronica beccabunga

Golden club (Orontium aquaticum)

Carex elata *'Aurea'* (Bowles golden sedge)

Lobelia cardinalis *'Queen Victoria'*

MARGINAL PLANTS (4)

The plants on these two pages present additional examples of the exciting variety of shapes – and textures – you can dot around your pool.

The choice of shapes and colours among the flowers and foliage of marginal plants is so varied that planning your pool can be as much fun as interior decorating. Marginals with bright green feathery foliage contrast superbly with the shiny, arrowhead-shaped leaves of plants such as the Virginia arrow

Virginia arrow arum
(Peltandra virginica). *The interesting arrow-shaped leaves will grow 30cm (12in) long and 15cm (6in) wide. It can become invasive so keep it in check.*

Cotton grass
(Eriophorum angustifolium)

Hemp agrimony
(Eupatorium cannabinum)

Myrtle flag or sweet flag
(Acorus calamus 'Variegatus')

Mimulus luteus *'Nana'. The flowers appear throughout the summer months.*

arum (*Peltandra virginica*), the beautiful heart-shaped leaves with purple undersides of *Ligularia dentata* 'Desdemona', the giant banana-like foliage of *Lysichiton americanus* (shown on page 43) or the elegant flat straps around the lovely blooms of iris. They all contrast perfectly with smaller-leaved marginals, such as *Geum rivale* and the marsh marigold (*Caltha palustris*). The tall spiky plants include grasses and sedges that prefer their roots to be waterlogged and are useful in natural water gardens because they bind together the banks of streams and ponds.

Above: Cyperus longus (*galingale*). *The dark green, grasslike, spreading foliage, which grows up to 1.5m (5ft) in height, bears attractive reddish-brown tufts in summer.*

Caltha palustris *'Alba' has rounded leaves and large buttercup flowers.*

Carex pendula, *a decorative native sedge.*

Galingale (Cyperus longus)

Geum rivale *makes clumps of green divided leaves and tiny orange flowers.*

Pennywort (Hydrocotyle vulgaris). *The shoots creep out onto the water.*

Mimulus luteus *bears larger flowers than M.l. 'Nana'.*

MARGINAL PLANTS (5)

Don't just go for the more spectacular plants; you need something occupying the lower levels, and there plenty of smaller ones to choose from, many of which produce attractive flowers.

The smaller-leaved marginals might not be as dramatic as the giant moisture-loving plants, such as rheum and gunnera (featured on pages 66–7), but they have equal value within your water feature, especially if you plant them in massed groups of a single species for extra impact. This way, smaller leaves and flowers are not over-looked in larger pools.

As a rule, smaller marginals grow quickly in damp mud, many of them providing quick ground cover to disguise and soften the banks and edges within a single season. Although smaller, the foliage is attractive and most produce pretty flowers, too, such as the spreading monkey musk, *Mimulus guttatus*. This hardy annual self-seeds readily to produce a carpet of small oval leaves along the edges of ponds and streams. In spring, you cannot beat the sight of bog arum, *Calla palustris*, with its white arum-like flowers and heart-shaped leaves. In summer, the yellow flowers of creeping Jenny (*Lysimachia nummularia*) appear among the dense, spreading, pale green carpets of foliage – quite different from the taller *Lysimachia thyrsiflora*.

Above: *In midsummer, Mimulus guttatus produces a mass of yellow orchidlike flowers with rust-coloured blotches.*

Euphorbia palustris

Sagittaria sagittifolia
'Flore Pleno' (Japanese arrowhead)

Typha stenophylla

Left: Sagittaria sagittifolia, *the common arrowhead, grows happily in or near the water's edge and is prized for its striking arrow-shaped foliage. This hardy plant also produces three-petalled white flowers with purple centres in summer.*

The giant reedmace (Typha latifolia) produces distinctive soft brown pokers.

Sparganium erectum

Lysimachia thyrsiflora

Water plantain (Alisma plantago-aquatica)

Potentilla palustris

Hypericum elodeoides

49

MARGINAL PLANTS (6)

Finally, here is a selection of plants whose shapes might be just what you need
to fill in the odd gap or corner of the edges of your pool.

The environs of a successful water feature need careful planning if plants are to look natural together and the shapes and colours are to be harmonious. When choosing marginal and moisture-loving plants, your first consideration, after selecting the correct light or shade and soil requirements, must be height and size. Decide which vantage points the pond or pool will be viewed from and select your plants accordingly. Restrict taller, spiky plants to the back of the pond and use the rampant, ground-covering species to smother the banks or beds towards the front. Exercise this element of design control even when planning a slightly wild, informal type of pool, and allow access to the water by not planting all the way round. This is not purely for the purposes of plant maintenance, but also to allow you to enjoy plants and wildlife at closer quarters. You may have to keep some of the more prolific species in check to maintain the desired effect. Among your marginal plant selection, try to achieve a good contrast of shapes and shades using different foliage effects, as well as blooms. With marginal plants, that contrast can be quite dramatic, as many types in this group have strong architectural qualities. Add seasonal interest with plants that flower at different times of the year. There are even a few species that put on a display at the end of summer when their leaves change colour or they produce interesting seedheads.

Above: Deciduous
perennial Colocasia esculenta,
*or taro, is grown for its bold,
strongly marked foliage. It
forms a close mound of pointed,
heart-shaped dark green leaves.
This plant is tender and is only
suitable for frost free pools.*

Left: The upright, cylindrical stems of bulrush
(Scirpus *sp.*) growing in the water provide
an attractive backdrop to the broad leaves of
Hosta crispula *thriving on the damp pond edge.*

Left: Typha minima *is ideal for the shallow edges of smaller ponds. It has slender green foliage so fine it almost looks like grass, and bears distinctive brown pokers in late summer.*

The marsh marigold (Caltha palustris) is a must for every pond. It produces an abundant display of bright yellow flowers in early spring and summer. There is a white version ('Alba' – shown on page 47) and a yellow form with double flowers ('Flore Pleno').

Typha minima

Glyceria maxima 'Variegata'

Rumex sanguineus

Zebra rush (Scirpus zebrinus)

Saururus cernuus

MOISTURE-LOVING PLANTS (1)

Certain kinds of plants always give the impression that water is nearby and planted in naturalistic swathes bring to mind a stream or lakeside. These are usually plants with grassy or strap-like leaves or broad, lush foliage. Use them to help create the illusion of a bubbling spring by surrounding a shallow depression filled with cobbles.

There are many interesting plants that flourish in moist but well-drained soil and they look perfect when planted to create a lush profusion of flowers and foliage near, or leading away from, the pond edge. Some are marginal plants that will tolerate damp but not totally waterlogged conditions, and these can be used in either position. Many are simply hardy garden perennials that you may already be familiar with from your herbaceous borders, and which prefer a moist, rich location. Others look the part but will actually tolerate drier conditions – at least on a temporary basis. This gives you plenty of scope to devise a suitable background planting plan for your particular pond or water feature, one that will blend readily into the rest of the garden or patio design.

Above: *Perennial* Anemone rivularis *is a good ground cover plant in damp areas. Its deeply divided green leaves are studded with white flowers with yellow centres in late spring and early summer. This plant will flourish in an area with damp soil and grow to a height of about 60cm (24in).*

Cowslip (Primula veris)

Primula x 'Geisha Girl'

Day lily (Hemerocallis)

Primrose (Primula vulgaris)

Left: Day lilies, Hemerocallis, bear beautiful but brief-lived lilylike flowers among deep green straplike foliage. This one is 'Pink Damask'.

Iris sibirica
Sparkling Rose'

Right: Japanese flag, Iris ensata *(or* I. kaempferi)*, is a beardless iris with large flowers, each measuring 7.5–15cm (3–6in) across. There is also an all-white form ('Alba') and one with variegated leaves (I. ensata 'Variegata').*

53

MOISTURE-LOVING PLANTS (2)

Moving slightly away from the pool, you would expect to find a variety of moisture-loving plants. If there isn't a natural wet edge you can always create suitable conditions artificially.

Moisture-loving plants are ideal for maintaining that poolside look, where there may not be a natural wet edge – in patio gardens, for example, or where the pond has a butyl or concrete liner. Because most of them grow prolifically given the right conditions, and as the majority have striking flowers or foliage (or both), they are an eye-catching part of the feature and have a wonderful softening effect on pond or stream edges, even in a patio location.

Below: During early summer, hardy Primula japonica *produces tall stems of dark red flowers rising above dense clumps of pale green leaves.*

To create the right effect around a small patio pond surrounded by paving, you can plant several of these lush species in pots or containers and position them in close groups near the water. Keep the containers well watered and mulch them in dry weather. Where you do have access to soil or planting beds, it helps to make sure that the soil is rich in humus to keep it damp and to mulch well to prevent moisture loss. If you cannot keep the soil damp, you will have to choose those plants that tolerate drier conditions or create a bog garden or marsh area as described on pages 94–95.

Above: The globeflower, Trollius x cultorum *'Canary Bird', with its dazzling display of bright yellow blooms, is one of the heralds of spring along streams and ponds.*

Trollius chinensis
'Golden Queen'

Primula vulgaris floreplena
'Ken Dearman'

Primula
denticulata

Geranium sanguineum

Primula denticulata

Heuchera
'Pewter Moon'

Left: The tubular red flowers and fleshy green foliage of Primula pulverulenta 'Inverewe' make a fine upright display in early summer.

Above: The distinctive white and yellow, buttercup-like flowers of Caltha palustris 'Alba' always look pretty at the edge of a pool.

55

Right: Lobelia cardinalis is prized for its deep red flower spikes and bronze foliage.

MOISTURE-LOVING PLANTS (3)

Check carefully how tolerant different plants are; some can only take a certain amount of moisture, while others tolerate it very well, others grow happily in sunshine or shade.

Since the range of plants included under the description 'moisture-loving' is so incredibly large, it pays to check exactly which conditions each plant prefers, so that you are sure of putting it in the right place within your overall planting scheme. Some of the moisture-lovers will thrive equally well in moisture-retentive soil or on the marginal shelf; others will not survive for long if the soil is a little too waterlogged, as the permanently damp conditions will cause their roots to rot.

There are plants that can surprise you; artemisias, for example, generally prefer drier conditions, but *Artemisia lactiflora* is a native of meadowland and stream valleys and will do well in damp soil. Check, too, whether your chosen plant prefers a sunny or shady position, as this can also drastically affect its chances of success. Some, such as *Lysichiton* and *Hemerocallis* will tolerate both sunshine and some shade.

Left: With its fluffy heads of creamy-white flowers in midsummer, meadowsweet, Filipendula ulmaria, is a favourite choice for informal pool edges and bog gardens.

Astilbe 'Straussenfeder'

Aquilegia
'Nora Barton'

Aquilegia alpina

Above: *Astilbes make an excellent display of feathery plumes along pond margins and boggy borders. Like* Astilbe x ardensii *shown here, they appreciate a little shade.*

Above: *Joe Pye Weed,* Eupatorium purpureum, *is a useful, tall perennial that produces heads of pink flowers during late summer and early autumn. The terminal flowerheads are borne on stems that can grow up to about 2.1m (7ft).*

Ligularia dentata 'Desdemona'. *This will also thrive as a marginal plant.*

Achillea millefolium 'Cerise Queen'

Lysimachia nummularia *'Aurea'. Also fine as a marginal.*

MOISTURE-LOVING PLANTS (4)

Consider planting ferns, aquilegia and some of the more
dramatic varieties of dogwood around your pool.

Plants that will tolerate a moist, waterlogged soil can be successfully planted close by the pool edge or in a specially created bog garden. A bog or marsh area might be used as a complementary extension of the pond edges or, if you have no other kind of water in the garden, installed as a separate feature in order to grow a selection of these often dramatically lush plants. You might consider the prolific umbrella plant, *Peltiphyllum peltatum*, whose large parasol leaves grow up to 30cm (12in) across. There is also a dwarf variety for smaller gardens. Most ferns will thrive in the moist soil of the shadier side of the pond or bog garden, while for a blaze of seasonal colour there are many free-flowering sunlovers to choose from, including the stately purple loosestrife, *Lythrum salicaria*.

Geranium phaeum

Primula rosea

Left: *The summer snowflake,* Leucojum aestivum, *actually flowers in spring, when it makes a welcome display of delicate white flowers and dark green stems.*

Right: *In contrast to the larger-leaved, lusher water plants,* Aruncus dioicus 'Glasnevin' *has delicate fernlike foliage and plumes of attractive white flowers during the summer months.*

Aquilegia longissima
McKana hybrid

Ligularia
przewalskii
'The Rocket'

Aquilegia vulgaris
(variegated form)

Above*: The striking autumn red foliage of* Cornus alba *'Sibirica' is deep green in late spring, when creamy-white flowers appear.*

Above*: If pruned, the Siberian dogwood,* Cornus alba *'Sibirica', produces a splendid display of bright red shoots in winter.*

Right*:* Ligularia przewalskii *'The Rocket' produces loose clumps of striking yellow flower spikes that provide late summer interest around the margins of the water garden.*

MOISTURE-LOVING PLANTS (5)

Other categories of plants don't mind damp soil as long as it is well drained.
Such plants include hostas and ferns.

Hosta *'Sun Power'*

If you can provide a rich, damp but well-drained soil, there are many delightful plants to choose from. Consider the pretty meadow flowers for the sunny sites, and woodland beauties for shady corners. For foliage interest, most ferns prefer a moist shady site and many hostas grow well in partial shade. Use the sun-lovers to make a brilliant border to be reflected in the water surface on bright days. The planting scheme can lead off into the rest of the garden and drier flower beds beyond. Blend astilbe's feathery plumes with the elegant iris, the butter-yellow, ball-like blooms of the globeflower, *Trollius* (shown on page 54), or with a selection of the many spring- and summer-flowering primulas, with their jewel-like colours and thick velvet foliage. For a superb display later in the year, the kaffir lily, *Schizostylis*, produces a show of freesia-like blooms in shades of red, white or pink. The small blue flowers of *Sisyrinchium bellum* also last until autumn.

Left: *Provided you can keep the slugs and snails at bay, hostas thrive in moist shady conditions and make a superb display of thick quilted foliage. Hosta sieboldiana, shown here, is one of the largest, with generous heart-shaped leaves with an almost blue tinge.*

Iris innominata
'Irish Doll'

Iris innominata
'Jack o' Hearts'

Iris hoogiana
'Hula Doll'

Lamium
maculatum
'White Nancy'

Sisyrinchium
bellum

Above: Sometimes called cuckoo flower or lady's smock, pretty Cardamine pratensis makes a show of delicate lilac flowers in spring.

Right: Hostas can offer many interesting colour and pattern variations. Hosta fortunei aureomarginata, as its scientific name reflects, has golden yellow borders to thick green leaves.

MOISTURE-LOVING PLANTS (6)

Plants that grow well in shade are invaluable, and even though
they are not out in full sun they are still capable of lighting
up the area with bright flowers and foliage.

Moisture-loving plants that prefer, or at least will tolerate, a little shade are invaluable for those shady areas around the pool or in the corner of the garden or patio where other plants will not thrive. It is worth seeking out a few such species to avoid ugly gaps or sickly specimens of plants that would rather not be in the shade but out in the sun, where they would thrive. Look out for woodland plants, such as *Astilbe chinensis* 'Pumila', that make good ground cover and produce rose-coloured flower spikes in summer in moist, shady places. Bistort, *Polygonum bistorta* 'Superbum', will tolerate dense shade and grow prolifically, making a carpet of tall leaves and pokers of tiny pink flowers by early summer. Many have striking foliage, such as the variegated figwort, *Scrophularia auriculata* 'Variegata', with tall green leaves splashed with cream.

Above: The giant reed, Arundo donax, *makes an elegant clump of tall, flag-like foliage up to 6m (20ft) tall in moist soil. The smaller variety, 'Versicolor', has creamy-white stripes along the leaves.*

Above: Bistort, Polygonum bistorta *'Superbum', grows well in damp conditions and makes a mass of pale pink pokers that are popular with bees throughout the summer.*

Bergenia crassifolia

Dactylorhiza maculata

Achillea ptarmica
'The Pearl'

Schizostylis coccinea
major

Astrantia
major

Alchemilla
mollis

Above: Parnassia palustris *thrives
in wet soil and full sun, producing
beautiful upturned white saucers
in late spring and early summer.*

Left: *Clump-forming knotweed,
Polygonum amplexicaule
'Atrosanguineum', produces a
blaze of tiny red flower spikes in
late summer.*

Right: *The water figwort,* Scrophularia
auriculata *'Variegata', forms clumps of
cream-splashed green foliage that is useful
for lighting up damp areas in semi-shade.*

MOISTURE-LOVING PLANTS (7)

It is worth familiarising yourself with the moisture-loving plants that are
also versatile enough to cope with the occasional dry spell.

In areas near or around the water feature, where the soil may occasionally dry out, there are a few lush-looking plants that prefer a moist position, but will usefully tolerate temporarily dry conditions. Save these for those spots where you know you will not be able to maintain permanently damp soil. These might be the outer limits of your poolside planting scheme or the pots and planting beds of a patio water garden. *Hemerocallis*, the day lily, is very adaptable and will withstand quite dry conditions. Hostas are also more tolerant of drier soils than you might expect, provided they have some shade. For areas that stay moist, the ferns are an ideal group to investigate.

Matteuccia
struthiopteris

Polystichum
setiferum

Phalaris
arundinacea

Brunnera
macrophylla

Athyrium filix-femina
'Frizelliae'

Above *White-striped gardener's garters,* Phalaris arundinacea *'Picta', grows prolifically in damp soil.*

Left: *The unfurling fronds of the striking fern* Dryopteris filix-mas *create interesting patterns as they catch the light. This native of marshy areas will provide a splendid display in a bog garden.*

Right: *The royal fern,* Osmunda regalis, *prefers a waterlogged soil but will tolerate sun and shade. It produces a magnificent display of fronds up to 1.8m (6ft) and 90cm (3ft) across.*

Asplenium scolopendrium
'Marginatum'

Geum chiloense
'Mrs J. Bradshaw'

Geum borisii

Dryopteris filix-mas
'Crispa Cristata'

Sensitive fern
(Onoclea sensibilis)

MOISTURE-LOVING PLANTS (8)

One of the most exciting aspects of having the opportunity to grow moisture-loving plants is the wonderful selection of dramatic large-leaved species that thrive in the naturally damp conditions.

The lush effect of even one of these plants can quickly and effectively fill a corner, make a focal point, or help to create the impression of a jungle of foliage. They contrast perfectly with other, smaller marginal plants, such as iris or primulas. There are plants such as the ornamental rhubarb, *Rheum palmatum*, for example, with spectacular bright green leaves that grow up to 90cm (36in) across. These magnificent five-lobed leaves create a stunning effect in the garden. Small white flowers appear in early summer borne on broad panicles. The plant might reach 1.8m (6ft) tall. Equally dramatic is *Gunnera manicata*, the largest-leaved plant that you can grow in garden conditions, with each cut-edged leaf capable of growing up to 1.5m (5ft) across. Both these outsize plants will grow in shade or sun. The many other plants with large – but perhaps not quite as dramatic – foliage include the Japanese butterbur, *Petasites japonicus*.

Right: *Glossy green Rheum alexandrae hides its creamy flowers behind large greenish-white bracts in early summer. These later turn red.*

Ornamental rhubarb
(Rheum palmatum)

Above: Rodgersia pinnata 'Superba' is popular along the banks of lakes and pools, as much for its handsome foliage, often tinged with bronze, as for the mass of starry pink flower spikes it produces in midsummer.

Gunnera manicata.
A superb architectural plant for a spacious location. Notice the flower spike among the central leaves.

Above: Another moisture-loving plant with both attractive leaves and flowers is Cimicifuga racemosa. *The leaves are deeply divided and bright green, the summer flowers a mass of bold white pokers.*

SMALL WATER LILIES

Don't get carried away with buying large water lilies, as they can take over
a small pond or pool. Choose ones of an appropriate size and
enjoy the scents and colours they offer.

For many pond owners, the large lily pad leaves and beautiful lotus-like blooms of the water lily are the epitome of a water garden. There is such a wonderful variety of types, offering different colours, forms and even scent. However, it is important to choose varieties with care, as the large vigorous types are totally unsuitable for smaller pools.

For the smallest ponds and tub and barrel gardens there are miniature lilies with a spread of about 30cm^2 (12in^2) and these need a depth of water of only 10–23cm (4–9in). Slightly larger, and ideal for small to medium-sized pools, is the group classified as 'small lilies', which have a spread of up to 0.3m^2 (3ft^2). They require a planting depth of 15–38cm (6–15in). You can grow these smaller types on the marginal shelf or in plastic baskets, but make sure that the crown is well below ice level to prevent frost damage. The miniature varieties will need adequate protection in winter in cold climates.

Whatever the size of the pool, remember that water lilies serve a very practical purpose as well as a decorative one: the spread of their leaves covers a large part of the water surface, offering shade and shelter for fish, and depriving algae of light and heat, without which they cannot reproduce too rapidly and give you problems with green water. Do not forget that there is as much variety in the foliage of lilies as in the blooms, with many different shapes, colours and markings.

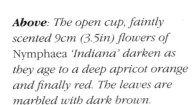

Above: *The open cup, faintly scented 9cm (3.5in) flowers of Nymphaea 'Indiana' darken as they age to a deep apricot orange and finally red. The leaves are marbled with dark brown.*

Right: *Nymphaea pygmaea 'Helvola'. This delightful miniature variety bears canary-yellow, star-shaped flowers throughout the summer months.*

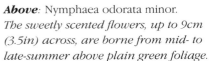

Right: Some water lilies, such as
Nymphaea caroliniana *'Nivea'* produce
beautiful semi-double flowers. These
are pure white and have a lovely
scent. The pale green, deciduous
leaves are also attractive.

Above: Nymphaea odorata minor.
The sweetly scented flowers, up to 9cm
(3.5in) across, are borne from mid- to
late-summer above plain green foliage.

OTHER SMALL LILIES

pygmaea 'Alba' (white)
'Laydekeri Liliacea' (pink)
'Laydekeri Purpurata' (red)
pygmaea 'Rubra' (red)
candida (white), 'Ellisiana' (red),
'Froebeli' (red), 'Aurora' (copper
yellow turning to salmon orange,
then red), 'Robinsoniana'
(vermilion/orange)

69

MODERATE WATER LILIES

In spite of a lack of overall size, lilies of more modest proportions offer sights and smells to compete with the rest of them.

Choosing the right size lily for your pool is one thing; selecting the correct number of varieties you might reasonably grow in the space is another matter. It is easy to be tempted by too many different types, and lilies will not grow well if they are crowded. Alternatively, they will swamp the water surface.

It can be difficult to calculate exactly how many plants you should allow yourself, as size and vigour vary considerably. Your water lily stockist should be able to estimate the final size of your chosen plant. As a general guideline, you can cover about 40 to 50 percent of the water surface, assuming that about 10 to 30 percent will be covered with

Above: *The pale orange and apricot blooms of* Nymphaea 'Sioux', *up to 13cm (5in) across, darken with age.*

Left: Nymphaea 'Rose Arey' *is one of the most colourful lilies. Its scented cerise blooms, with their starlike petals, display bright orange stamens tipped with yellow, and the purple leaves turn to green.*

other floating plants. The moderately sized water lilies suitable for small to medium pools usually require a planting depth of 15–45cm (6–18in) and will cover about 0.6–1.1m² (6–12ft²).

After several years, these lilies may start to outgrow smaller pools. If you lift and divide them, this will reduce their growth and provide them with fresh nutrients.

WATER LILY PROBLEMS

Lilies can suffer from lily beetle or blackfly. Remove badly affected leaves and use a fish-safe insecticide or hose them into the water for the fish to eat. Crown rot may affect newly planted lilies; remove any affected plants for treatment.

Above: Nymphaea 'Firecrest' is aptly named; the centre of each pretty pink bloom blazes with a cluster of golden stamens, streaked with orange and red, like tiny flames. This variety is ideal for small to medium pools.

Left: Nymphaea 'Sultan' has deep red blooms that fade to pink as they reach the tips of the petals. The cluster of stamens is a warm golden colour and the large flat leaves are a dark green.

Above: Nymphaea 'James Brydon' is prized for its crimson-pink peony-like blooms and purple leaves, which turn to dark green with a brown edge. The cup-shaped flowers have a delicate scent.

MEDIUM WATER LILIES (1)

It is worth considering medium-sized water lilies not just for average-sized pools, but also for larger water features where you might choose two medium lilies instead of only one of the larger, vigorous types. In that way, you could enjoy several different colours and types.

This extensive group of lilies requires a planting depth of 6–24in (15–60cm) and each plant can be expected to make a spread of foliage up to 1.1–1.3m² (12–15ft²).

As with the other hardy water lily groups, you will find a superb range of colours to chose from among the blooms, as well as a great range of forms, from star shapes to large double forms. As well as the classic shades of snow-white, lilies are available in every shade of pink, from hot cerise to pale rose. There are really eye-catching deep red lilies, golden yellows and even copper-orange varieties that change colour as they age. Often, you will find that lilies are not an even colour all over, but that the shade is densest towards the centre of the bloom, fading almost to white at the tips of the petals. This subtle colour gradation only adds to their delicate charm.

Above: Nymphaea 'René Gérard' is one of the most popular lily varieties, especially valued for its free-flowering habit. It has particularly large blooms. The pointed petals are a deep rosy red at the centre, fading to pale pink flecked with a deeper pink towards the tips.

Left: Known for its reliability, Nymphaea 'Marliacea Albida' grows vigorously and is free-flowering, producing plenty of large, white fragrant blooms among the contrasting dark green foliage.

Above: For intensity of colour, you cannot beat Nymphaea 'Escarboucle', whose large, long-lasting blooms are a stunning shade of crimson. The plant produces a mass of blooms throughout the flowering season.

Right: Nymphaea 'Pink Sensation' is a relatively new introduction. Its pointed petals fade from a deep pink at the base to a silvery pink at the tips. The dark green leaves have an attractive bronze tinge.

Above: The cup-shaped, pale pink blooms of Nymphaea 'Formosa' are stippled with darker pink, and reach 9.5cm (3.75in) across. Faintly scented.

MEDIUM WATER LILIES (2)

Here we look at a further selection of medium water lilies, the most popular
type for the majority of garden pools. Bear in mind that lilies
like plenty of sunshine, and are also hungry plants
that need to be well nourished.

Water lilies prefer a warm, sunny position, as their blooms tend to be smaller and paler when they grow in shade. Depending on the climate and levels of sunshine, most plants should start flowering as temperatures rise above 18°C (65°F) in early summer, the blooms opening in the morning and closing later in the afternoon. You may find that if the weather is particularly warm, the flowers will open earlier in the morning and close in the early afternoon.

The blooms are often smaller and paler when the plant is young; in an older plant, poor flowers are more likely to be an indication that the plant is potbound or needs a dose of fertilizer. With such a greedy root system, lilies need large containers with plenty of rich aquatic potting mixture.

Left: Nymphaea 'Marliacea Rosea' is a deeper pink variety of the vigorous N. 'Marliacea Carnea'. It flowers white for the first year or so and then a rose-pink stain spreads up into the petals from the base of each bloom.

Right: For a really showy display, Nymphaea 'Mrs. Richmond' has huge blooms that are pale rose-pink on opening, deepening to a darker pink with age. The leaves are light green.

Above: *Nymphaea odorata 'Alba' is a free-flowering medium-sized variety with pure white, cup-shaped blooms and a delicious scent. The bright apple green foliage is equally attractive.*

Above right: *The blooms of Nymphaea 'Attraction' are a deep wine colour at the base of the central petals, graduating to almost white at the tips of the outer petals once established.*

Right: *Nymphaea 'Moorei' is similar to the popular N. 'Marliacea Chromatella', but is not quite as large or free-flowering. It has pretty primrose-yellow flowers spotted with brown. The foliage is spotted with purple on the undersides of each large leaf.*

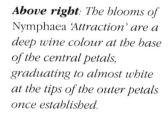

LARGE WATER LILIES

Large, vigorous water lily species really do need plenty of space, as they can spread
to cover an area of anything around 1.3–2.3m² (15–25ft²)
and require a water depth of 23–120cm (9–48in).
They would quickly clog up smaller pools.

Once established, any size of water lily will reward you with a succession of flowers through the summer, each bloom lasting three to five days before sinking below the surface.

As well as having a strict preference concerning levels of sunshine and needing plenty of rich soil in order to flourish, water lilies dislike any disturbance of the water, so they are not suited to pools with a fountain or waterfall. If there is a slight flow of water through a natural lake or pond, you should be careful where you position your lilies and preferably plant them in containers that are easy to lift out of the water, so that you can reposition them elsewhere if necessary. You can then check the water lily stems to make sure that they are not slowing down the flow of water or encouraging silting up.

Above: Once the plant is established, Nymphaea 'Conqueror' bears large, wine-red blooms flecked with white. The petals become paler towards the tips. This is one lily that, unusually, stays open in the evenings.

Right: N. 'Alba' is the classic white lily native to Europe and Asia. Its growth habit is so vigorous that it is really only suited to larger lakes and pools, where it makes a spread of mid-green flat leaves and cup-shaped blooms with bright yellow centres.

Above: Nymphaea 'Charles de Meurville' blooms early and has a long flowering season. It produces outsize wine-red flowers, each one up to 25cm (10in) across. The outer petals may be paler, opening to reveal a mass of golden stamens.

Left: Vigorous Nymphaea 'Colonel A.J. Welch' is excellent for deep water. It has large, star-shaped, canary yellow blooms with narrow pointed petals. The flowers are not plentiful, but they stay open later in the afternoons.

Right: Large white globular blooms with prominent green sepals identify Nymphaea tuberosa 'Richardsonii'. It is an improved form of a native North American lily and is suited only to larger pools. The large round leaves are an attractive apple-green colour.

Plants in a variety of shapes, sizes and colours produce an eye-catching display in a bog garden.

THE PROJECTS

MAKING A BUBBLE FOUNTAIN

Fountain features make striking and unusual additions for a container garden.
Team a bubble fountain, like the one shown here, with 'potted ponds'
of different sizes to make a complete patio water garden.

A fountain in a pot is the ideal way to add moving water to a display of potted 'water lily ponds', since these plants cannot be grown under fountains – they do not thrive if the tops of their leaves keep getting wet. And in a garden used by small children, a feature filled with pebbles where there is no standing water – however shallow – is a safer option.

Be sure to set up a potted fountain carefully. The container must hold enough water so that the submersible pump is constantly covered with water. Adjust the jet so that the water trickles back into the pot and is continuously recycled – if too high, much of the water will go over the sides of the container, which will soon empty itself until the pump runs dry and is damaged. The reservoir of water will, in any case, need topping up at least once a week, since natural evaporation will gradually lower the water level. Make sure that the stones and pot, plus other ingredients, are all perfectly clean when you set the feature up – any dirt and grit will soon clog the pump. And remember that electricity and water make a dangerous combination, so consult a qualified electrician if you feel the slightest need for practical guidance.

You can buy pebbles or cobbles in various sizes from a garden or aquarium centre.

1 *For a potted bubble fountain, you will need a large plastic pot, a plastic hanging basket that fits inside it upside down, a small submersible pump and smooth pebbles.*

2 *Make a hole in the base of the plant basket so that the nozzle of the fountain fits tightly when pushed through it. Keep pushing the nozzle through until both the rim of the basket and pump are flush.*

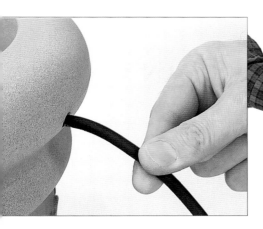

3 *Drill a small hole, just big enough to take the wire from the pump, right under the lip of the pot where it is less visible and will be above the water level. Thread the wire through the hole and reconnect it to the plug at the other end.*

4 *Lower the pump into the bottom of the pot and lodge it firmly in place.*

5 *Put a ring of the largest pebbles around the edge of the plastic hanging basket to keep it in place. The basket is now acting as a cover for the pump.*

The bell fountain is a good spray pattern for outdoors, as the wall of water stands up to a breeze. A fountain that makes a fine spray has tiny droplets that blow away, creating a one-sided effect.

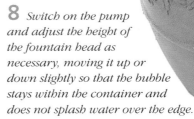

6 *Part-fill the pot with water until you can just see the level. The aim is to provide sufficient water in the base to feed the pump as it returns through the stones. Continue filling the container with smooth pebbles. Leave the pump nozzle exposed.*

7 *Fit the fountain head over the nozzle. Various types are available that will give a bell fountain effect, as here, or a spray pattern. Use more pebbles to hide the base of the tube.*

8 *Switch on the pump and adjust the height of the fountain head as necessary, moving it up or down slightly so that the bubble stays within the container and does not splash water over the edge.*

81

MAKING A LOG ROLL RAISED POOL

This raised pond, based on a large, strong rigid plastic container, is the quickest and easiest way of making a water feature. It makes a striking and unusual centrepiece for a patio, tiny courtyard garden or a themed garden within a garden.

Being small and self-contained, this pond can be dismantled in a few minutes and moved. This alone makes it an asset for a small garden water feature, and is ideal for anyone planning to move house in the near future who wants to take their pond with them.

The basic idea is extremely flexible and can easily be adapted to suit many different styles of garden. The log roll used here can be bought ready-made from a garden centre or made from timber offcuts. For a designer look, use planed timber and a coloured water-based wood stain, as here, that will team well with matching coloured trellis in a modern garden. Using rough, bark-clad timber, the pond acquires a natural woodland style that would go well with potted ferns and hostas to add sparkle to a shady spot. For an ultra-modern effect, substitute the log roll with a sheet of mirror acrylic bent around the container to form a complete cylinder. You could use outdoor adhesive to glue mosaics or pebbles to the outside of the container, or even apply acrylic paints to create a mural on a sheet of flexible plastic bent around the pool.

For a more traditional effect, try building a surrounding dry stone wall or use bricks; unless the wall is to be used as seating, it is not essential to cement the stones together, so the pond remains portable.

Unlike many potted ponds, this one holds quite a large volume of water, making it practical to include fish, plants and even a normal water lily suitable for a small pond instead of one of the real miniatures. But do not mix fish and/or a water lily with a fountain in such as small space, since the turbulence created by the fountain will not suit the fish, and waterlilies will not grow where their foliage is always getting splashed.

Stipa
tenuissima

Chamaecyparis

Cyperus
involucratus/
alternifolius

Bergenia

Hedera helix
(*variegated ivy*)

1 *As an alternative to a preformed pool shape, you can use any large, strong, rigid plastic container like this to make a formal style pond. It should ideally be black.*

2 *Encircle the container with log roll. The roll should be the same height as the container; saw it to size if necessary, then treat it with coloured wood preservative. Stand the container in its final position before filling it with water. Position the log roll around it when the paint is dry.*

3 *In early spring, fill the tub with water to about 15cm (6in) of the rim, to allow for displacement when you add the plants and pump. Let the water stand for a few weeks before adding the plants.*

4 *Place a clean plastic flower pot or net pond pot upside down in the bottom of the container, close to one side, to raise your water plant to the correct level in the tub.*

5 *Cyperus enjoys standing in water. Sit it on top of the upturned flower pot. The top of the rootball should lie just below the water level when the tub is full.*

6 *Add a small, low-voltage submersible pump. It can sit on the floor of the pool as there will be little sludge inside. Add water to within 2.5cm (1in) of the rim. Adjust the fountain head until it is flush with the water surface, and alter the flow rate so that it produces a gentle gush of water.*

WINTER CARE

Where the water will not freeze solid in winter, this pond can be left outside all year round. Alternatively, unplug the pump in winter and replace it with a small electric pond heater to prevent the water freezing. Otherwise, bale out about half the pond water to reduce the weight and move the container carefully under cover for the winter; an unheated conservatory, car port or frost-free greenhouse should be sufficient protection in all but the very coldest areas, but good light is essential.

ADDING A WATERFALL

A waterfall or cascade is an excellent way to add movement – and, if necessary, height – to your garden scheme.

Above: *An informal-style cascade built up from slabs of stone needs a liner beneath it to prevent the water soaking into the surrounding soil.*

A waterfall need not be large and, indeed, if were too tall it would require a tremendous volume of water and a very powerful pump to keep it circulating. Even a trickle from one formal patio pool into another slightly below it makes a delightful feature, both from the point of view of the attractive background sound as well as the visual appeal it provides. A rocky waterfall cascading over boulders into an informal pond is the perfect backdrop and a useful device to utilize waste stone and soil from your pool excavations.

You will need a pump powerful enough to cope with the volume of water and the height of the falls; if you have already installed one of the larger types to run a fountain or other moving water feature, it may be possible to employ the pump to run both features by adding a T-piece to the outlet pipe. Your pump stockist should be able to advise you on the size and type of pump. If the waterfall is a big one, you may also need a top-up tank to maintain a large enough water supply.

You can buy preformed fibreglass waterfalls that you can conceal behind boulders and plants to create the impression of a series of natural-looking cascades.

Below: *In this setup a submersible pump supplies water to a spray fountain and a waterfall. Make sure that the pump you choose can power both outlets.*

Here the tubing has been left exposed to show where it runs. In your garden you can hide the tubing so that the water appears to spring from the stones.

SETTING UP A PUMP FOR FOUNTAIN AND WATERFALL

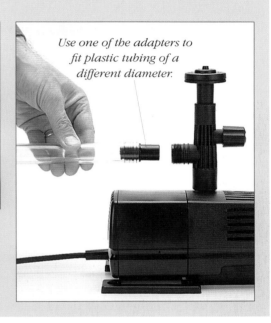

Use one of the adapters to fit plastic tubing of a different diameter.

1 *Remove the blanking cap. Push on plastic tubing to supply the waterfall. This tube has a bore of 25mm (1in).*

2 *Use the adjuster to control the flow of water. Fully screwed in, all the water will go to the waterfall; fully out, and the flow will split both ways.*

The maximum size of the fountain depends on the height of the waterfall and the length of tubing involved.

WATERFALL ONLY

If you just want to run a waterfall, simply connect a suitable length of plastic tubing directly to the outlet of a submersible pump (as here) and direct the water flow as you wish.

PLANTING OXYGENATORS

Follow these simple steps to get your oxygenating plants established in the pond, but make sure you keep an eye on them as they are capable of spreading out of control.

If you have a layer of soil at the bottom of your pond then oxygenators can be simply planted by weighting the stems with a small metal weight, or some similar device such as a small stone, and dropping them into the water so that they become established. However, rooted types are best planted in plastic baskets, which makes them easier to maintain. Should the plant become too rampant, you can simply lift the basket and trim back the plant as required before replacing the container in the water.

Use the aquatic soil specially formulated for water plants.

Because oxygenators grow so prolifically, especially during the warmer months, they will need keeping in check, especially at the end of the summer. As a guide, you should not allow oxygenating plants to take up more than one third of the pool's volume or they will start to become as much of a problem as the green strands of blanketweed. In any case, it is a good idea to thin out your plants before they start dying back for the winter.

Propagating oxygenating plants is equally straightforward. If you need more young, fresh plants, simply propagate them by dividing the bunches as shown on pages 122–123.

1 *One container with specially perforated sides will be sufficient for up to eight oxygenating plants, depending on the size of the pool. Use a trowel to fill it with potting mix.*

2 *Fill the container almost to the rim. Use a dibble or your finger to make a sufficiently large planting hole for each plant.*

3 *Insert the first oxygenator into the planting hole and gently spread out the roots. Pack more potting mixture around the plant and firm it in carefully with your fingers.*

Use clean washed gravel and avoid any minerals that might affect the water chemistry.

4 *Continue adding the rest of the plants you have chosen, planting them in the same way and positioning them evenly around the container.*

Elodea canadensis

Elodea crispa

Potamogeton crispus

Callitriche hermaphroditica (C. autumnalis)

Fontinalis antipyretica

Ranunculus aquatilis

5 *When all the plants are firmed in, top up the container with a layer of gravel or small stones to anchor the potting mix and to prevent fish from rooting out the plants.*

6 *The finished container is ready to be lowered into the pond or pool. Should the plants become too rampant, simply lift out the container and cut back the plants as necessary.*

7 *Once the plants are established in the basket they will soon start to spread out below the surface of the water in the pond.*

87

THE PROJECTS

PLANTING A MARGINAL

As long as you can keep their foliage clear of water, marginals are
fairly straightforward to plant, and if you use a container
it is easy to move and maintain them.

Marginal plants will thrive with their roots submerged in water but their foliage must be free of the water surface. It is important to plant them quickly, so that their roots and stems are exposed for as short a time as possible, and you must plant them at exactly the same level as they were in the pot or nursery bed.

Remove the plants carefully from their container, but not until you have everything ready to plant, otherwise the roots may suffer. If you are planting in a bog or marsh area (you can use many marginals as bog plants), all you do is simply dig a hole about four times the size of the rootball, water the

The finished container ready to be lowered onto the marginal shelf of the pond. When filled with soil, plants and gravel, it is quite heavy.

Fill the marginal basket with moist aquatic potting soil.

Keep the plants moist and in their original pots until you use them.

1 *Remove the marginal plant gently from its pot, taking care to support the stem loosely between your fingers.*

Make sure that the topdressing of gravel is clean and washed.

88

2 *Position the plants carefully in the container. Two or three plants of the same species will make a good display. Backfill and firm in.*

plant well and lower it gently into the hole, making sure it is at the right level. Replace the soil (enriched with organic matter if necessary) and firm in the plant. If you have a 'natural' pond with soil submerged around the edges, you can plant directly on the marginal shelf by backfilling with a suitably rich, water-retaining soil. Hold the plants in place with large rocks or boulders.

For pools with 'clean' marginal shelves you can use special containers that you can lower onto the shelf and lift out for easy maintenance. These containers are available in various sizes suited to single specimens or several plants together. Curved baskets are ideal for the marginal shelf that is positioned around a circular pool.

3 *Finish filling the container with aquatic soil and level the surface. Add a layer of gravel so that the potting mix does not float away.*

4 *Holding the container firmly by the handles on both sides, lower it gently onto the marginal shelf without disturbing the water too much.*

5 *The marginal basket is in position on the shelf with the plants visible from the pool edge. It is easy to lift the container out for maintenance.*

PLANTING MARGINALS IN A WOODEN BARREL

Marginal pond plants make fascinating container subjects. Any container that holds water is suitable, but a wide half-barrel is best as it has a large water surface that makes the most of the plants' reflections – one of their best assets.

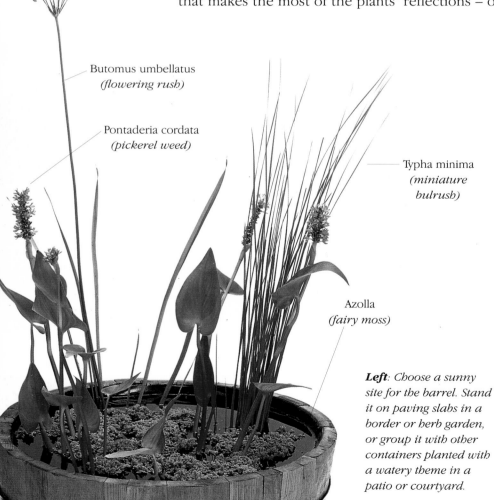

Butomus umbellatus
(flowering rush)

Pontaderia cordata
(pickerel weed)

Typha minima
(miniature bulrush)

Azolla
(fairy moss)

Left: *Choose a sunny site for the barrel. Stand it on paving slabs in a border or herb garden, or group it with other containers planted with a watery theme in a patio or courtyard.*

Marginal plants are the sort that can be grown in 0–30cm (0–12in) of water (measured over the top of the pot). This includes all the popular water irises, marsh marigolds and rushes, as well as many of the

1 *Line the tub with butyl pond liner. Drape the material loosely inside and arrange the slack in folds. Put 2.5–5cm (1–2in) of well-washed gravel into the bottom of the tub to bed the marginal plants into later. Half-fill with water to weight the liner down into the bottom of the container. Rearrange the folds so that surplus material is evenly distributed around the edge.*

2 *Use sharp scissors to trim away the excess liner, leaving enough spare to allow for turning over the edge. Make small tucks to even out large folds in the material around the rim of the barrel.*

3 *Turn the liner edges under, smoothing out tucks in the material to flatten them down as you work. Use waterproof tape, ideally black, to secure the liner firmly inside the rim of the container.*

plants commonly grown as bog garden plants, such as zantedeschia. Avoid plants that merely grow in damp soil; although they are sometimes sold mistakenly as marginal plants, subjects such as hosta and astilbe do not enjoy standing in water above their necks and do not last long under these conditions.

Marginal plants are often imposing specimens that grow very quickly; to keep them at a suitable size for a half-barrel, lift them out and divide them every spring, just as they are starting into growth. This is good for them and will help keep their size manageable. Once planted up, keep the barrel topped up with water. Remember that in hot weather it can lose 2.5cm (1in) of water each week through evaporation.

4 ***Right****: Begin adding plants; choose a mixture of striking flowering and foliage marginal plants that contrast well in shape. Upright, reedlike shapes are typical of many waterside plants. This is* Typha minima *(miniature bulrush). Leave the plants in the net-sided pond pots that they are growing in when you buy them.*

6 ***Below****: Top up with water to the rim of the container and check that the tape holds the edge of the liner firmly. Finally, float a handful of azolla over the surface. In full sun, this lacy-leaved plant turns bright red. Alternatively, use other floating plants, such as water lettuce or water hyacinth.*

5 ***Right****: Pickerel weed has striking heart-shaped leaves and blue flowers from early mid-summer to early autumn. It works well with the tall linear leaves of the other plants. Three plants are enough, as they will make quite a bit of new growth over the summer.*

PLANTING A CONTOUR BASKET USING A LINER

Special planting baskets for use in pools come in a wide range of sizes and shapes to take one or several marginal or aquatic plants. Since you do not want to be fishing them in and out of the water too frequently, the sensible thing to do is to take the time and trouble to plant them up correctly in the first place.

When you have selected the correct size of basket, it may need lining to prevent the soil washing out through the perforations into the water. This also makes it easier to remove the plants, should that prove to be necessary at a later date.

When it is finished, the container, complete with damp soil, plants and pebbles, will be heavy, so lower it with care; never drop it even a short distance or you will disturb the water and possibly damage your liner. If you cannot reach comfortably by leaning over, get into the water if necessary to manhandle the container into position.

It is important that baskets are positioned at the correct level for the plants' usual depth requirements. In deep water they may need propping up on bricks or blocks.

Baskets should only need lifting when the plants have become too rampant and either •require thinning or replacing.

This plastic lining material will allow water into the basket but will not rot away when immersed.

1 *If you use a large-weave basket, you will need to line it first with hessian or woven plastic liner to prevent the potting mixture washing away into the water. Tuck the liner into the basket but do not trim it yet.*

2 *Press the liner material lightly and evenly into the container. Now you can start filling the basket with a suitable aquatic potting mixture.*

3 *Remove the plants from their pots and position them in the basket, making sure that they are at the correct planting depth and are standing upright. These are marginal plants.*

4 *Carefully backfill and top up the basket with potting mixture, firming in the plants as you go.*

5 *Add a layer of small stones or gravel to keep the potting mixture in place once the container is submerged.*

Iris laevigata
'Variegata'

Zantedeschia
aethiopica

6 *When the container is planted, trim away any excess liner using a pair of sharp scissors.*

7 *This is the finished container, lined and planted and ready to be lowered onto the marginal shelf.*

CREATING A BOG GARDEN OR MARSH AREA

You don't have to live in a damp, low-lying area to have a bog garden – all it takes is some pond liner and imaginative planting to turn your pool side into a luxuriant oasis. Add the sound of trickling water and the illusion is complete!

To create a bog garden or marsh area you need to excavate the desired area to a depth of about 35cm (14in), cover it with a large sheet of punctured butyl or other pond lining material and fill it with water-soaked soil. Ideally, there should be water standing about 5cm (2in) on the top. It is important to keep the area poorly drained and to make allowances for fluctuations in the water level according to the differing levels of rainfall throughout the year. In a naturally boggy site this is not a problem, but where you have created the environment artificially, you will need some kind of overflow facilities. This is easily installed where the bog garden adjoins a pool area by providing a few holes (about 1.25cm/0.5in in diameter) in the dividing wall. For this two-way top-up drainage system to work, the bog area should represent no more than about ten to fifteen percent of the total surface area of the pond. If there is no pond next to the bog garden, then you can install overflow facilities into a nearby ditch. The easiest way to top up the

moisture levels in a dry spell is to insert a length of punctured plastic pipe at the construction stage. If you conceal the exposed end of the pipe among the plants in the bog garden you can easily trickle in more water as and when required.

Right: A bog or marsh area offers the chance to grow a selection of exciting marginal plants, such as hostas, iris, typha, mimulus, phalaris and violas.

1 *For your marsh or bog area you will need a hole which is going act as your moisture reservoir. If there is not already a natural depression in the ground, begin by excavating the area to a depth of about 35cm (14in).*

2 *Roughly level the base of the hole and prepare the surface for the liner. Don't worry about sharp stones since the liner will be punctured deliberately later on.*

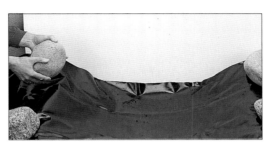

3 *Spread a large sheet of pond lining material over the area. You can use butyl rubber or a less expensive PVC-based type of liner.*

4 *Anchor the liner securely in position by placing a few large, smooth boulders around the edges that will not tear the material.*

5 *Puncture the bottom of the liner a couple of times with a garden fork, for aeration.*

6 *Spread a layer of washed gravel over the lining at the bottom of the bog area. This will help the soil to retain moisture once it is established.*

7 *Lay a section of perforated pipe on the gravel in the bottom of the excavation. Allow the end of the pipe to protrude.*

Make irrigation holes in the pipe 30cm (12in) apart.

8 *With the irrigation pipe in place, fill the area to the original ground level with a rich, moisture-retaining aquatic planting mixture.*

9 *Soak the ground thoroughly, so that about 7.5cm (3in) of water remains on top of the soil.*

PLANTING UP THE BOG GARDEN

The key to success is to think bold! Plant in swathes of one kind
of plant to mimic wild vegetation and use one or two carefully placed specimens for dramatic impact.
In this relatively small space, the highlights are provided by hostas. A larger garden
could accommodate ornamental rhubarb or even a gunnera.

Here we show how to plant up the bog garden created on pages 94–95. The beauty of creating a bog or marsh area in the garden is that it offers you the chance to grow a wider range of exciting marginal plants. Or you may welcome the chance to establish a rewarding water feature without the need for expensive excavation work. Ideally, the site should be sheltered from prevailing winds with a little, but not too much, shade. The most natural position is adjoining the banks of an informal pond or pool, but if you are planning an individual bog garden, then any slight depression or poorly drained area will make an ideal site. You should try to avoid

3 *Some marginals, such as this hosta, offer wonderful shape and colour possibilities simply in their foliage. Remember to protect these plants against the attentions of slugs and snails.*

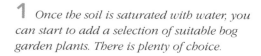

1 *Once the soil is saturated with water, you can start to add a selection of suitable bog garden plants. There is plenty of choice.*

2 *Position the plants in the ground so that they are at the same depth as they were in their pots or nursery bed. Firm them in well.*

positioning your bog garden too near any tree roots as they tend to drain moisture from the soil. If your garden is small or unsuitable, you can still enjoy a miniature bog garden created in an old stone sink or barrel, provided there are three or four drainage holes and a good layer of crocks in the bottom. You can grow one or two moisture-loving plants in each container as long as you keep the soil saturated; mulching with pebbles helps to reduce moisture loss. The containers can stand on the patio or in the garden; a series of tubs containing different plants and sunk to their rims in a bed of gravel looks particularly effective. Or arrange several old sinks on the patio at various levels.

4 *Do not hesitate to arrange clumps of a single species, here Primula veris, to create an impact as a foil to more delicate-looking bog plants.*

5 *Fill in any spaces between the new plants with washed pebbles to reduce moisture loss and to create an attractive background.*

6 **Below:** *Aim for a variety of shape, size and colour in your plants to produce an eye-catching display throughout the growing season.*

Mimulus

Lysimachia thyrsiflora

Astilbe

Lobelia cardinalis

Primula veris

Hosta

A BOG GARDEN IN A TUB

Bog garden plants make ideal subjects for containers. This is a good way of growing them if you garden on dry soil, where they would not be happy in the open ground. It is perfect for a small garden, since many bog garden plants are large and invasive, spreading rapidly given a free root-run, so that they soon become a nuisance.

Lobelia cardinalis
'Queen Victoria'

Lobelia syphylitica

Milium effusum *'Aureum'*
(Bowles' golden grass)

Zantedeschia aethiopica

Houttuynia
cordata
'Variegata'

Caltha
palustris
alba

Lysimachia
nummularia
'Aurea'

Use a watertight container; if yours has drainage holes in the bottom, or if it leaks, simply line it with butyl rubber pond liner or heavy duty black plastic before filling and planting. Since the soil will be kept permanently damp, this type of container suits all sorts of bog garden plants, including houttuynia and *Lobelia cardinalis*, as well as border plants that enjoy moist to boggy conditions, such as hostas, lythrum and astilbe. Since space is limited, restrict yourself to plants with a long summer flowering season and those with good architectural foliage. Those with both, such as zantedeschia, are doubly valuable.

Bog garden plants are often sold growing in special net-sided pond pots. They are best left in their pots; the roots are intended to grow out through the sides so that you can lift them out later if they grow too big and you want to replace them. Otherwise, the whole container becomes over-run with roots, and you have to empty the whole tub and replant it all at once.

Left: These plants will thrive in a sunny spot on a patio or by a pond. They die down in winter but come up again the following year.

1 *Line a large half barrel with butyl pond liner, loosely cut to shape, and put half a bucketful of washed gravel in the bottom.*

2 *Fill the container to just below the rim with pond planting mixture, or garden soil with a high clay content but no added fertiliser.*

Zantedeschia aethiopica *(arum lily) grows 45cm (18in) high and makes a bold statement in the middle of the display.*

3 *Place a tall plant at the back. This striking Lobelia cardinalis 'Queen Victoria' produces spikes of red flowers in mid- to late summer.*

4 *Choose plants that contrast well. Use drooping or trailing plants round the sides and shorter plants towards the front to make the best display in a small space.*

5 *Add a trailing plant at the front; this is a gold-leaved form of creeping Jenny, Lysimachia nummularia 'Aurea'. Top up the soil level to within 2.5cm (1in) of the rim. Add at least a full watering can of water, leaving the soil nice and boggy.*

6 *Leave the barrel for about 30 minutes, then water it again if the soil has absorbed so much moisture that the surface is no longer boggy. Level it roughly and scatter 2.5cm (1in) of washed gravel over the surface. Decorate with a small cluster of attractive pebbles.*

7 *Now that the weight of the soil and water have pulled the liner down into the barrel, trim the excess butyl liner with sharp scissors. Roll the edges over and tuck them out of sight below the gravel.*

PLANTING A WATER LILY

Water lilies need to be planted with care, as they need plenty of room and will feed voraciously throughout their lives. Think carefully about where to put them, as they can become very heavy and difficult to move once they have become well established.

Water lilies are greedy feeders, especially the more vigorous types, so they appreciate the largest container you have room for and a soil depth of at least 15cm (6in). Containers come in various types and sizes, including the familiar perforated baskets specially designed for aquatic plants, but also as wide, solid-sided bowls.

Spring is the best time to transplant lilies, as they will have just started their growing season and this gives the plants plenty of time to establish themselves before becoming dormant. A reasonably mature specimen could be expected to flower in its first season, although the first blooms may be smaller and paler than expected.

It is important not to cover the growing point of the lily tuber or rhizome. The crown should stand proud of the soil or gravel.

Lower the heavy baskets carefully to the correct level, using bricks, blocks or upturned baskets as supports. Start young plants near the water surface – allow, say, 15–25cm (6–10in) over the crown and lower them gradually as sufficient leaves develop. As a guide, you should not be able to see open leaves below the water. It may be several years before you can fully lower deep water lilies to 90cm (3ft) or more.

1 *Left: The latest lily baskets have louvered sides with special perforations that do not require lining. Start to fill the container with a suitable aquatic potting mixture.*

2 *Carefully lay the lily onto the potting mixture and begin to top up the basket with more mixture, firming in the plant as you proceed.*

3 When the basket is full, cover the surface of the potting mixture with gravel or small stones to keep the soil in place once the basket is lowered into the water. The layer of small stones will also help to prevent fish from disturbing the plant.

4 The finished container is ready to be lowered into the pool. Return the plant to water as soon as possible after planting to ensure its survival.

Make sure that the crown of the plant is above the level of soil in the basket.

5 Place sufficient bricks in the pool to bring the basket to the required level below the surface of the water. See plant label for planting depth. Lower the container carefully into the water so that it rests securely on the bricks. Do not drop it in; you may damage the plant and pond liner.

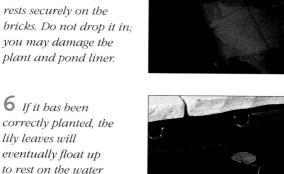

FEEDING WATER LILIES

Once the lilies are established, they will begin to deplete the natural resources in the planting mixture and will benefit from a regular feed.

Water lily food comes in powdered, tablet or sachet form; simply press this into the top of the basket. Follow the manufacturer's instructions.

6 If it has been correctly planted, the lily leaves will eventually float up to rest on the water surface. Place young plants in shallow water at first.

Fertilizer in small bags

Powdered fertilizer

CREATING A MINIATURE WATER LILY POND

If you do not have room for a conventional pond,
then a potted pond could be just the answer.

Put the container in position first, as it will be difficult to move once filled. You can use normal tap water but if possible fill the tub and allow it to stand for 48 hours before introducing plants. This allows much of the chlorine to disperse.

When choosing plants, opt for those with a long season of interest. A single miniature

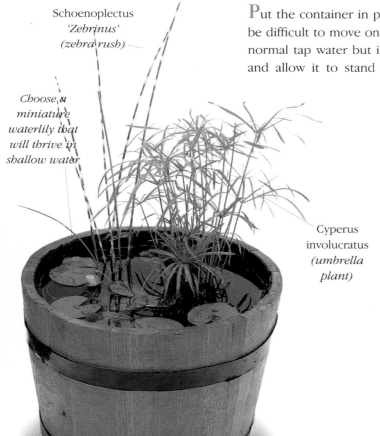

Schoenoplectus 'Zebrinus' (zebra rush)

Choose a miniature waterlily that will thrive in shallow water

Cyperus involucratus (umbrella plant)

1 *Use a waterproof wooden barrel, or line it first with thick black plastic or butyl rubber pond liner. Half-fill it with water and add a tall, strikingly shaped, leafy plant.*

2 *Choose a second plant that complements the first; foliage types look good all season. Slowly submerge the planting baskets until they sit on the bottom of the tub.*

3 *As there are going to be fish in the pond, add a spray of Canadian pondweed, Elodea canadensis, to oxygenate the water Being evergreen, it keeps working in winter, too. Anchor the clump down with a clean pebble.*

water lily could be used alone; it will quickly fill a 45cm (18in)-diameter barrel with foliage, and flowers all summer. Or add up to two other plants, as we have done here. Choose good foliage plants to contrast with the lily; go for bold architectural shapes that will look good all summer.

Or why not make a group of potted ponds? Use matching containers in various sizes, each with a different planting theme. You might have a water lily pond, a marginal plant pond of water irises, zebra rush and miniature bulrush, a potted bog garden, a 'pond' of fountain and pebbles, and a floating garden of water hyacinth, azolla and water lettuce.

If you want fish, choose the largest container possible and only a few small fish, or there will not be enough oxygen in the water for them. Make sure that the fish have plenty to eat and keep the water clean for them. If you decide to add further plants later on, do not forget about the fish!

4 *Top up the pond to just below the rim of the barrel. Now there is only the water lily to plant; if the barrel is overfilled at the start, water will spill over the edge each time a new plant is added, so take care.*

5 ***Right****: Lower the water lily slowly, protecting the leaves and flowers, which become weak and floppy out of water. They easily tear if snagged on the edge of the barrel. Stand the pot on the bottom of the barrel. After a few hours, the lily leaves shrug off water and emerge floating on the pond surface. Water lily flowers only open fully in direct sun, so make sure the pond is correctly sited from the very start.*

6 *Four small fish are plenty for a barrel this size. Float their bag on the surface for 30 minutes so that their water reaches the same temperature as that in the tub.*

7 *Open the bag underwater and allow the fish to swim out in their own time. Tipping them out might injure or frighten them.*

103

CREATING A WATER FEATURE IN A BARREL

If you would really like a pond feature, but have no room in the garden or on the patio, or if excavations and major building work are impractical, you can always set up a miniature pool in a pot, tub or other suitable container.

Provided they are scaled down, you can have all the features you set your heart on; water lilies, marginal plants, fish and even a tiny, sparkling fountain. The finished tub can be a real focal point and provide hours of pleasure for very little outlay in terms of time and money, as well as space. Any waterproof container is suitable, from a large cut-down barrel to a small terracotta or plastic patio pot. The only real proviso is that the chosen container has not been treated with any poisonous or fungicidal chemicals that might damage plants and fish. Some garden centres sell tub kits that come complete with everything you need, even a selection of plants, to be assembled at home. Alternatively, you can buy a ready-made bubble fountain in a stone or terracotta container, with plants and pebbles installed for an instant and very attractive moving water feature.

1 *These are the ingredients to make a stunning water feature in a tub. It is a good idea to set out what you plan to include in the final display before you start work. This also gives you the chance to see whether the elements will look good together.*

2 *Since the wooden barrel is not waterproof, the first task is to line it. Use a large piece of proper pond liner and push it firmly down inside. Leave plenty of liner overlapping the edge of the barrel as the liner will settle down once water has been added. Smooth the liner out with your hands, pressing it into the bottom.*

Make sure this tube is firmly pushed into the pump

3 *Next put the pump into the barrel. This is a small, mains-powered model ideally suited to the size of the display. Carefully place a brick, or maybe two bricks if the barrel is deep, in the base of the barrel, being careful not to damage the liner. Place the pump on the brick for stability and to bring it up to the correct height.*

4 *Place a layer of bricks around the inside of the barrel. These will provide platforms to support the plant pots and stones. Use hard bricks sold for paving; they are a lot more durable in water.*

5 *Add some cobbles to fill in the spaces between the bricks. These will help to stabilize the piles of bricks and will also stop the pump moving around once the feature is operating. Once again, take great care not to damage the liner as you place the cobbles in the barrel and move them and the bricks into suitable positions.*

6 *Now add the large stones that will form the visible part of the feature. Rounded boulders such as these not only look attractive but will also stand continuous immersion in water. Stones like these are now widely available at garden centres and DIY stores. Never remove them from beaches or other natural sources.*

7 *Add water until it reaches the base of the boulders. This will leave enough expansion room to add the plants and final stones. Be careful not to overfill the barrel: you still have a lot of material to add in.*

PLANTING UP A BARREL

Here we show how to plant up the barrel prepared on pages 104–105.
Of course, all kinds of troughs, pots, tubs and barrels are suitable for planting up
in this way. Just make sure that they are painted inside with a sealant or lined with
butyl rubber or plastic pond liner to ensure that they are watertight.

Do remember that once filled with water, a few plants and any other water features you may choose, such as an ornament or fountain, the tub or pot is going to be extremely heavy, so decide on its final position while it is empty and plant it up in situ. If you are going to have to move the feature, place the container on a low platform with lockable casters for mobility.

A water feature in a tub makes an excellent focal point for a dull corner of the garden or patio, where it might be raised on such a platform or a few bricks for extra prominence. Alternatively, stand it on a bed of pebbles or gravel or surround it with large stones and pots of lush plants to reinforce the watery effect. To show the tub at its best, make sure you position it against a suitable backdrop, such as a wall, fence or plain greenery. Large pebbles or a wall behind are also useful for installing concealed spouts for moving water effects to enhance the feature.

1 *If you want to neaten things up a bit at this stage you can trim off more of the liner. The weight of the water will have pushed the liner into its final position.*

2 *Now begin to add the plants. Since they will be immersed in water, you can choose from a wide range of marginal plants that thrive in these conditions. Pot them into the plastic mesh baskets that you use for the pond.*

Smooth stones or boulders look best in small pools.

3 *If the display has a definite front view, then plan the planting with this in mind. Adding this low growing water forget-me-not towards the front will work well with the tall water buttercup at the back of the barrel.*

4 *Once the planting is complete, you can add more stones to fill in spaces that seem to 'appear'. Adding another boulder here creates a better display. Be careful not to dislodge the outlet pipe of the pump as you move heavy items around.*

5 *Add cobbles and pebbles to match the colour range and shape of the boulders. This helps the feature to look more like the bank of a natural stream. By now the barrel is very heavy and you should be working on it in its final location in the garden setting.*

Ranunculus flammula

Lysimachia thyrsiflora

Iris versicolor 'Blue Light'

Myosotis palustris

Epimedium x youngianum *'Roseum'* (Not a marginal but would look attractive close to the barrel.)

6 *This is the final display with a three-tier spray fountain head fitted to the pump. The edges of the liner have been trimmed neatly around the top of the barrel.*

Primula veris (Not suitable for inside the barrel, but this bog garden plant thrives in damp soil.)

7 *If you prefer a bell-shaped effect then fit the appropriate head. Be careful not to pull out the central tube of the pump when changing heads.*

WATER PLANTS IN METAL BUCKETS

Shiny metal buckets make superb containers for waterside plants.
Arrange them close together to create a 'themed' display. A background of pebbles,
gravel, water or a reflective surface such as glass would be ideal.

A group of shiny metal containers of different shapes and sizes, planted with marginal and bog garden plants, looks good in an informal cottage-style garden, outside a back door, or by an outbuilding. Stand the display on a base of gravel, cobbles or pebbles; it works well in front of a pond, a large glass door or a white-painted wall where sunlight will be reflected between the various surfaces to create a sparkling effect.

Suitable plants include those that grow naturally in shallow water or boggy ground that never dries out. To make a good display plant some containers with a single large specimen foliage plant and others with a group of smaller flowering plants, then team them together. All water plants associate well together but for a more 'designed' look, allow one colour, say yellow, to run through the scheme in each container. It only takes a small amount in each to link the display together visually, since they are already in matching containers.

Ideal plants would be compact or slow-growing subjects with a long flowering season. In practice, however, few water plants fall into this category. It is best to choose plants with as long a flowering season as possible, and either plant them out in a damp part of the garden after one season in containers, or else divide and replant them the following spring.

PLANTING UP A METAL TROUGH

1 *Part fill the trough with good quality potting mix. A shallow trough with waterloving plants needs no gravel drainage.*

2 *Choose a mixture of upright plants with contrasting shapes, textures and colours, but of roughly similar height. Knock them out of their pots and plant them in a row.*

GROWING INVASIVE PLANTS IN BUCKETS

1 *Place a layer of clean gravel in the bottom ot a watertight bucket to give it a firm base and to support the finished display.*

2 *If the plant is large, stand it in its pot in the bucket. If it is small, fill the bucket with potting mix and plant as normal.*

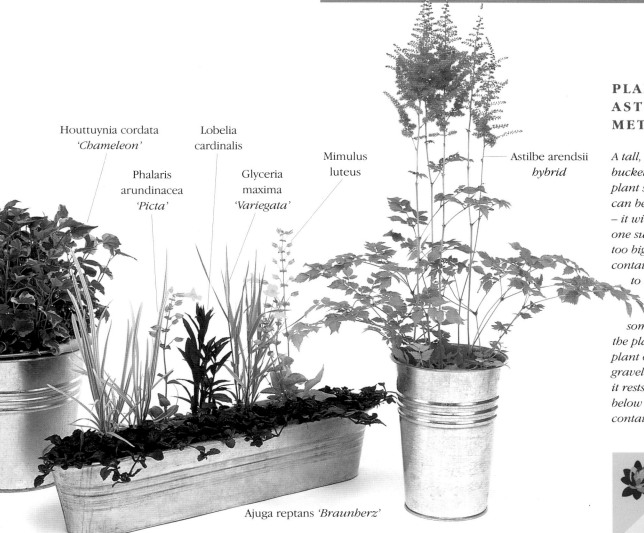

Houttuynia cordata 'Chameleon'

Phalaris arundinacea 'Picta'

Lobelia cardinalis

Glyceria maxima 'Variegata'

Mimulus luteus

Astilbe arendsii hybrid

Ajuga reptans 'Braunherz'

PLANTING AN ASTILBE IN A METAL BUCKET

A tall, narrow, metal flower bucket suits a tall, graceful plant such as astilbe. The plant can be left in its pot or removed – it will only be left in place for one summer as it will soon grow too big. Fill the base of the container with gravel to act as ballast to keep it upright, and to provide some drainage for the plant. Position the plant on top of the gravel bed, so that it rests 2.5cm (1in) below the rim of the container.

3 *Plant several of the same kind of low, spreading plant along the front and at each end of the container. Here we have used a purple-leaved form of ajuga.*

4 *Use a narrow trowel and a little potting mixture to fill any gaps between rootballs. Fill the trough almost to the rim, as the mix will sink when watered. Trickle water around each plant to settle the mixture around the roots. Add more water, leaving the mix wet but not sloppy. Keep it wet, as bog pants dislike drying out.*

SUITABLE PLANTS

Caltha palustris, Cyperus, Filipendula ulmaria 'Aurea', Hosta, Iris laevigata, Iris versicolor, Lysimachia nummularia, L. punctata, Juncus effusus 'Spiralis', Mentha aquatica, Mimulus, Schoenoplectus 'Zebrinus', Typha minima, Zantedeschia aethiopica.

NOVELTY WATER FEATURES (1)

Whatever the size of your garden, there is absolutely no reason why your water features should be confined to conventional tubs or barrels. A more interesting approach is to think 'if it will hold water, it could be a garden feature'.

A delightful miniature pond or water garden is easily assembled using a selection of scaled-down plants and features. The secret is not to choose too many of these or the effect will be overcrowded and lose some of its impact.

Provided the pool or tub is deep enough for a small fountain pump, you can devise all kinds of interesting moving water effects, from a simple jet to tiny bubbling and dome sprays. If you have small children, the reservoir can be concealed below a bed of pebbles or an old millstone. Alternatively, a wall-mounted spout or simple dish can make a simple but eye-catching, self-contained feature in the smallest of spaces.

Choose ornaments that are properly in proportion to your feature and position these close by the pool if not actually in the water. If you are more interested in plants, then there are many dwarf varieties to choose from, including miniature water lilies. Plants will probably need regular trimming to keep them in check.

Left: Where space is really limited, a wall-mounted water spout such as this is a delightfully elegant way of incorporating water into the garden without the need to install a pond or pool. You can buy these features in kit form at water garden centres.

Right: The sense of movement and the variety of shape and colour in the wet stones are the simple ingredients that give this tiny bubble fountain feature its huge appeal.

Above: A simple planting scheme combined with an unusually detailed mosaic fountain base give this small circular pool maximum impact. This would make a good feature in any garden.

Above: An old barrel, partially sunk into the ground, makes an excellent miniature pond that might be sited anywhere in the garden or on the patio.

Right: Japanese garden designers are the masters of small moving water features like this shishi-odoshi, originally designed to scare deer from the garden. With its gentle trickling and regular 'tock' as the pivoted bamboo hits the rock, this relaxing feature could form part of an oriental area with bamboos and Japanese-style ornaments.

NOVELTY WATER FEATURES (2)

Any number of different containers can be used for garden water features, combined with a variety of different techniques. Here are some more ideas for brightening up the garden.

Given a little imagination, all sorts of novel water features are possible. Use them all round the garden to add detail and interest.

In a conservatory, a fountain feature adds a glitzy 'finishing touch' to a collection of exotic tropical plants. The moving water creates humidity that the plants will enjoy, while the sound suggests a tropical stream, adding ambience to the dramatic shapes of giant flowers and architectural foliage, and so contributing to the jungly illusion.

Outdoors, a simple fountain makes a good addition to a shady garden, as the moving water adds sparkle and reflects light; it looks particularly good amongst damp-loving plants, such as hostas, ferns and astilbes. For a more sophisticated grouping, team a classical fountain and statue with ivies and euonymus, or a helxine (soleirolia) 'lawn'.

A water feature in which the water gurgles over large pebbles, or that operates a bamboo 'deer scarer' (a regular feature of Japanese gardens) adds an extra dimension of sound to a garden designed primarily for relaxation, so you might consider placing one on the patio or close to a garden seat.

Another big attraction of water features is the variety of garden wildlife that comes to bathe and drink. If using water in a deep container, such as a tub, make sure that these visitors are able to get out as well as in. Water features that do not involve standing water, such as fountains coming up through millstones or cobbles, are safest for both small children and wildlife. They also have the big advantage of not harbouring mosquitoes, which need still water to breed successfully.

Above: A pump makes an authentic feature for a cottage-style garden, and teams well with a display of marginal water plants in the larger barrel.

Left: The design of this blue bowl is very appropriate for a potted lily pond; use only the smallest miniature water lilies (Nymphaea pygmaea) *in this type of display. They will flower all through the summer.*

Above: Water features such as this millstone are safe to use as a feature in gardens where small children play unattended.

Right: Water features need not be highly sophisticated; this angled pipe running into an animal drinking trough works well with a display of plants that enjoy cool, humid, shady conditions.

Above: A touch of humour spices up even the plainest containers. A display like this is perfect for a shady corner as it makes you look twice – and the fountain adds light, sound and sparkle.

Above: The fountain causes the water in this jar to overflow constantly, sending a thin film of moisture down over the sides, from where it is caught in a reservoir underneath and recycled via a submersible pump.

CONTAINERS OF WATER WITHOUT PLANTS

A container of water on its own contrasts with surrounding plants, which might be grown in other pots or in the ground. Use running water for greater interest by installing a small submersible pump. To combat algae, you could add a liquid pond water treatment to the water in the pot, but may prefer not to do so if wildlife use the water. The best plan is to dismantle the pond at the end of summer before the first frosts, and scrub everything clean before putting it away for the winter.

Above: The lion's mask is a very popular fountain design. You could stand a small water plant in a pot in the trough underneath, or it would look just as good surrounded by decorative foliage.

Above: This stone pot overflows continuously through flanges in the sides. The water is then recycled from the collection container underneath the pot by a small pump positioned inside.

Left: Nymphaea 'Sultan' has deep red blooms that fade to pink as they reach the tips of the petals. Water lilies are easily propagated.

HELP!

115

LOOKING AFTER A POND

If you have planned and constructed your pond with care, there should not be much need to refer to this section of the book as in the main the pond should look after itself. However, you want such a central feature to look its best at all times, and there are measures you can take to improve conditions in your pool.

Left: *If you get the ecological balance right, both pool and water plants will flourish with minimum maintenance. It may take more than one season to be successful.*

Once established, a properly constructed and well-planned pond requires very little maintenance. Most water plants grow prolifically and are not prone to pests and diseases. Just keep an eye open for lily beetle or aphids on your water lilies and hose them into the water for the fish to eat. In fact, the plants in and around your pond will grow rather too well and thinning out and cutting back is one task you will have to tackle at least· annually. Take this opportunity to propagate new plants by taking cuttings or dividing roots.

If you have the ecological balance right in your pond, the water should basically look after itself. If not, and you get a spell of prolonged sunshine, it may turn green with scum – which is actually overactive algae. This is more of a problem with smaller pools; you can add chemicals as a short-term solution or install a water filter in the pond as described on pages 34–35.

Above: *Fish prefer clean water and plenty of cover for protection and shade. The plastic strings over the pool here are to deter herons, which can be a nuisance poaching your livestock.*

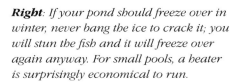

Right: *If your pond should freeze over in winter, never bang the ice to crack it; you will stun the fish and it will freeze over again anyway. For small pools, a heater is surprisingly economical to run.*

The actual pond construction should last many years without any need for repair. It is possible to mend cracks in concrete and rips in lining material using the appropriate repair kit, but the pond will have to be emptied and drained. Never do this at the end of the summer when pond life is just settling down to weather the winter.

Make winter care for your pond a routine. Remove any dead leaves with a rake or net at the end of summer, clear away any dead plant material to prevent it polluting the water and install a small pond heater if you are worried for your fish. Ponds deeper than 60cm (24in) should not freeze totally, so this will not be a problem.

A moving water feature, such as a fountain or waterfall, will also keep the water relatively unfrozen. If kept running permanently, you could leave a submersible pump in the pond during the winter. Otherwise remove and clean it and store it in a dry shed. Both submersible and surface pumps need a regular overhaul and should only be operated according to the manufacturer's instructions.

AVOIDING GREEN WATER

Green scummy water is the scourge of small ponds. You can avoid the problem if you keep the water free from dead or decaying plant material. Cover the pool with a net to catch falling leaves at the end of the growing season. Making sure the surface is partially covered by floating plants and water lilies helps shade out the light and heat that algae thrive on. If you are still getting problems, then you may have to install a biological filter.

Above: *Sunshine encourages algae, causing green scummy water.*

Right: *Twirl algal threads out on a stick.*

TRIMMING A WATER LILY ROOTSTOCK

In order to keep water lilies healthy and looking their best, it is important to trim their rootstocks periodically. Always use a sharp knife and keep water to hand to keep the rootstock moist, but do not be afraid to trim judiciously, as the plant will feel all the better for it later on.

Once you have the rootstock in your hands, you might find it useful to rinse the plant gently in cold water to remove the excess mud so that you can see more clearly what you are doing. It is important not to let the plant dry out while you are working on it, so have a watering can nearby to keep it wet.

Cut the rootstock with a sharp knife or scalpel blade to avoid bruising. Your first cut should remove the newest section of growth, which will develop and become established more quickly than one of the 'eyes'. Allow about 7.5–20cm (3–8in) of rootstock. Trim away most of the long anchoring roots from this piece, leaving just a few smaller roots to provide the plant with nutrients. Also trim off any dead tissue and most of the old leaves, since these will not grow and might make the plant too buoyant and even lift it out of the container. The new plant will produce fresh leaves and roots all the quicker for this rather drastic treatment.

You can slice or break off the 'eyes' on the discarded rootstock to propagate more plants, as shown on pages 124–125.

1 *Using a sharp blade and keeping the plant moist, slice cleanly through the rootstock to sever the new growth and create a fresh plant.*

2 *Remove the long anchor roots from the new plant, making a clean cut close to the crown. Leave the smaller roots intact.*

The original plant crown will form the basis of the new one.

These small white roots will develop and sustain the new plant.

3 *Removing the old roots encourages the plant to grow new, stronger ones, and will prevent the old roots rotting and infecting the crown.*

4 *Trim the leaves from the top of the plant in the same way. If left on, they will die back, putting the plant at risk from infection.*

5 *Gently plant the newly prepared lily crown in a perforated container of aquatic potting mix, using the same technique as for any new lily plant.*

The crown should be just proud of the soil and pebbles.

Severed anchor roots

6 *A layer of small stones sprinkled on the surface of the potting mix will help to keep the soil and the plants in place once they are submerged in the pond or pool.*

7 *The new plant is now potted up in its container and ready to be submerged in the pool or nursery tank until the lily has become established.*

PROPAGATING AQUATIC PLANTS BY CUTTINGS

Spring is the best time to take cuttings of plants in the water garden,
as they will have the growing season ahead of them to get established.

Rampant water garden plants tend to grow loose and leggy after a while and it is a good idea to maintain a continuous programme of propagating from existing plants each year. This way you can keep your display looking in peak condition at no extra cost.

Studying your plant will usually tell you if it is suitable material for taking cuttings. With plants grown in damp conditions, you will often find tiny roots along the stem near a node or leaf joint and this will make your job

1 *This aquatic plant has already started to produce roots from nodes along the stem and so is an ideal subject for propagation by taking cuttings.*

2 *Take hold of the fleshy stem at a point close to where a leaf node has started to make healthy root growth.*

3 *If you pinch sharply between finger and thumb, the required section of stem should come away in your hand.*

4 *Remove the leaves from the stem below the root growth by pinching them sharply and cleanly between finger and thumb.*

5 *Pinch off the top of the stem, too; this will give you another plant to propagate, even though there is no sign yet of roots on this section.*

6 *Again, remove the lower leaves from your section of stem to allow root growth to flourish.*

even easier. Spring cuttings tend to be what are called soft stem cuttings – that is, non-flowering shoots cut just below a leaf node and the lower leaves removed. By removing several sections from a single shoot, you can create several new plants from one stem.

Be sure to keep the cuttings misted until they have started new root growth. The new plantlets can be grown on in nursery beds or tanks of waterlogged soil – marginal species can often be grown in damp soil and introduced gradually to increasingly deeper water as the foliage grows taller. When they are fully established you can plant them out. You can swap new plants with friends as an inexpensive means of acquiring different varieties or use them in or around your own pool as required.

The small bundle of roots here will establish the new plant quickly.

7 *These two cuttings, prepared from a single small section of stem, are now ready for potting up. Do not leave them out of the soil for too long. Make sure that the cuttings are not damaged or affected by disease or plant pests.*

8 *Gently insert the cuttings into small pots of damp potting mixture and firm in. Keep well watered until good leaf and root growth are under way and then transfer them to the water garden.*

In moist conditions this cutting will soon produce new roots to support it.

PROPAGATING AQUATIC PLANTS
BY ROOT DIVISION

Root division is one of the simplest forms of propagation and since its primary purpose
is to reduce an over-large plant to more manageable proportions, it is
good for reviving the original specimen, too.

Again, spring is the best time to start digging up marginal or moisture-loving plants and splitting them up, giving new plants the summer months to establish new growth before they die back for the winter.

The type of plants suitable for root division will be established hardy perennials that have obviously become overgrown. If you dig them up and examine them carefully, you can often see from the rootball that the plant is in fact several plants clustered together. Breaking or pulling them apart is a simple job, although tough roots may need to be cut with a sharp knife. The technique involved is exactly the same as you would use to split up land-based garden plants.

Some water garden plants, such as iris, grow from thick rhizomatous roots that produce sucker shoots, and these are ideal for cutting into separate plants. (This technique is featured on pages 120–121.) Other water plants have tuberous roots that need to be carefully divided into shooted sections.

Above: *The bright splashes of red and cream on the green leaves of this* Houttuynia cordata *'Chameleon' make this a prized plant for adding welcome colour to the water's edge.*

Right: *One single specimen, such as the* Houttuynia *above, might yield as many as half a dozen new plants for the water garden. With care, each one will grow on strongly.*

1 *Start by filling sufficient small pots to hold your cuttings with a potting mixture recommended for moisture-loving plants. Water the pots well until the potting mixture is soaked through. Standing the pots in a plastic tray helps to reduce and contain the mess.*

PROPAGATING MARGINALS BY DIVISION

Some marginal plants grow from a tuberous rootstock, which is easy to divide. Dig up the overgrown plant using two garden forks and carefully split the roots or tubers to give established plants a new lease of life.

Make sure that each plantlet has a healthy growth of roots and that the foliage is free from damage or disease.

1 *Cut through the rootstock with a sharp knife to divide the original clump into smaller plants.*

2 *Hold the plant loosely in one hand and gently tease apart the rootball with the other, taking care not to damage the roots or stems. Set aside each plantlet ready for potting up.*

3 *Several separate plantlets should naturally come away in your hand. Handle them very carefully.*

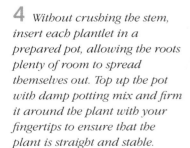

4 *Without crushing the stem, insert each plantlet in a prepared pot, allowing the roots plenty of room to spread themselves out. Top up the pot with damp potting mix and firm it around the plant with your fingertips to ensure that the plant is straight and stable.*

2 *As a bonus, you could create several new plants from the old root material. Each one of these should grow away healthily.*

PROPAGATING A WATER LILY

Water lilies can be expensive to buy, so if you have a mature specimen that is starting to heave itself out of the container, it is worth the trouble to propagate new plants from the old rootstock.

A lily will be fairly old and well established before it is suitable for propagation. Lift it carefully free of the water and lever or cut away the container.

There are two types of growth; those that produce a tuberlike rhizome that grows horizontally, and others that grow from a knobby upright rootstock. It is important to remember which type you have, because you must plant the rootstock at the same angle.

As well as being able to propagate plants from new sections of growth or side shoots on the old rootstock, you could propagate each small 'eye' – tiny budding plants that appear along the length of the tuber – to produce more than a dozen plants from a single old one. These small plantlets should become established within about two years.

1 *Using a sharp knife or scalpel blade, sever the main plant cleanly from its fleshy rhizome. It is a good idea to wear gloves when handling lily roots, as some species can stain your hands.*

Left: Nymphaea '*Marliacea*' is a good reliable lily bearing pretty pink blooms with a delicate scent throughout the summer. Water lilies come in many other shades.

Having taken out the 'eyes', you can now pot up this part of the plant, as shown on pages 100–101.

Each of these 'eyes' will grow into a complete new plant.

2 *Now, with your knife, begin removing all the sprouting 'eyes' along the rhizomatic tuber. Put the eyes carefully to one side until you are ready to pot them up. Each eye should come away cleanly. In some species, you will not even need a knife, as they break off easily in your hand. Take care not to damage the tiny 'crown'.*

3 *A single rhizome from a mature lily plant might yield as many as twelve to twenty new plants. This will be far more than you need, so swap with family and friends.*

4 *Press each new plantlet into a tray of moist aquatic potting mixture, leaving the 'crown' of the small plant exposed. Allow space for a layer of small stones to be added to stop the soil floating out of the tray.*

5 *A single tray can hold as many as twelve new plants. Each plant will take a couple of years to grow to a size suitable for planting out. The plants will need transferring to larger containers as they develop.*

6 *Cover the potting mix with small stones, taking care not to bury the small plants completely. Submerge the tray in a tank or a large bowl of water until the plantlets mature.*

Iris pseudacorus *'Variegata'*.
The flowers appear from
early to midsummer.

PLANT IDENTIFIER

ACORUS CALAMUS 'VARIEGATUS'

SWEET FLAG

The leaves and rhizomes of this hardy marginal plant resemble those of an iris, and it is often mistaken for one; however, its flowers show clearly that it belongs to the arum family. The deciduous, sword-like leaves are striped green and cream, flushed red in spring, and have a well-defined mid-rib. The flowers, borne towards the top of the stem, are carried in a densely packed yellowish spike 5–7.5cm (2–3in) long. The leaves release a pleasant scent when crushed, and they and the rhizomes have long been used in Asia for scenting toiletries and flavouring drinks and sweetmeats. Height: 60–75cm (24–30in); spread to 75cm (30in) in about 4 years.

APONOGETON DISTACHYOS

WATER HAWTHORN

Also known as Cape pondweed, this is a tuberous aquatic plant well suited to the larger pond, since it prefers water 30–60cm (12–24in) deep. It has long, oval, mid-green floating leaves, which it may retain in winter where the climate is mild, but generally loses in cooler areas. The plant is, however, fairly hardy and will survive all but the coldest weather in a dormant state.

From late spring through to autumn, white flowers with black anthers are held on a forked stalk just above the water. Like hawthorn blossom, they smell of vanilla, which may account for the common name. Spread: 45–60cm (18–24in).

ASPLENIUM SCOLOPENDRI

HART'S-TONGUE FERN

Ferns enjoy moisture, so they are excellent for planting close to a pond or in a bog garden. The evergreen hart's-tongue fern has broad, bright green, strap-like leaves that grow from the base of the clump and are smooth and shiny. In some varieties, such as 'Crispum', the leaves have waved and crisped margins, in 'Cristatum' they are branched and crested at the tips. Height 45–75cm (15–30in); spread 45cm (18in).

Hart's-tongue fern is good in limy soils and needs moist conditions and shade; it will even grow in a crevice in the rocks beneath a fall of water.

AZOLLA FINICULOIDES

FAIRY MOSS

BUTOMUS UMBELLATUS

FLOWERING RUSH

CALLA PALUSTRIS

BOG ARUM

Despite its name, this floating aquatic is not a moss, but a fern, with tiny lacy fronds only 5–7mm (3/4 in) long. These spread out over the water to form a dense mat, pale bluish green in summer, but turning red and brown in autumn. *Azolla caroliniana* is very similar in appearance. Neither plant bears flowers.

Fairy moss is best grown in a small pond so that the exuberant summer growth can be controlled by netting. If allowed to grow unchecked, it can rapidly overrun a pond and become a nuisance.

Azolla can be propagated simply by removing plants from the pond and separating them. It is killed by frost, but will usually survive in a dormant state.

A handsome, erect marginal plant, the flowering rush is indigenous to Europe, where it is found growing in water 2.5–23cm (1–9in) deep along streams and in wet marshlands. In cultivation, it is best suited to larger ponds.

The smooth, narrow, rush-like leaves are triangular and grow irregularly; they are bronze-purple when young, turning to a rich green as they mature. In summer, fairly large, pink three-petalled flowers are borne in umbels on long stems; a white-flowered form also exists. The plant dies back and becomes dormant in winter; it is hardy to −25°C (-13°F). Height: 60–90cm (24–36in); spread 50cm (20in) in 2–3 years.

A scrambling plant, as much at home in shallow water as in the muddy margins of a pond, the bog arum is useful for hiding the edges of a pond. The smooth, glossy, dark green, heart-shaped leaves, borne on long stems, are more or less evergreen. In spring, tiny, white papery spathes enclosing green and white spadices appear; they resemble those of the peace lily, *Spathiphyllum*. If the plant is pollinated – by water snails – clusters of bright red berries form. The bog arum prefers bright sun and is very hardy, requiring little care, except to cut back dead foliage in winter. Height 15–30cm (6–12in); spread 30–40cm (12–16in) after 2 or 3 years.

CALLITRICHE
HERMAPHRODICTIA

AUTUMN STARWORT

This is the form of the plant most frequently seen in cultivation, although starworts are commonly found in the wild throughout Europe and North America. It is a useful oxygenator in ponds in cold areas, since it is evergreen and hardy.

The bright green leaves, 1–2cm ($\frac{1}{2}$–$\frac{3}{4}$in) long, are held on long, thin stems and are usually totally submerged, but in summer they float to the surface in bunches and insignificant flowers appear. As well as being an excellent oxygenator, starwort provides a haven in which fish can lay their eggs and feed on the small pond creatures that collect among the leaves.

CALTHA PALUSTRIS

MARSH MARIGOLD

The marsh marigold or buttercup, also known as the kingcup, is a splendid waterside plant, which is also often seen growing in waterlogged woodland or meadows. It forms neat mounds of round, glossy, dark green leaves, among which golden yellow flowers, up to 2.5cm (1in) across, appear in early spring. It is one of the earliest aquatics to bloom and makes a good partner for the water forget-me-not, *Myosotis palustris*. The single form is most common, but 'Flore Pleno' is a double form, and 'Alba' is white. Height: 25–64cm (10–24in); 'Flora Pleno' and 'Alba' 25cm (10in).

CERATOPHYLLUM DEMERSUM

HORNWORT

One of the most reliable oxygenators, hornwort is found worldwide and is extremely hardy, growing well even in cold water. It seldom produces roots, but floats both at the surface and beneath the water. It has thin, brittle stems which are completely covered in whorls of dark green, bristly foliage. Fish find the stems attractive, since they offer some protection from predators and also harbour small aquatic insects, which they eat.

In warm areas, the plant is evergreen, but where winters are colder, the stems sink to the bottom of the pond in late autumn and overwinter as dormant buds, or turions, which produce new stems in spring.

DRYOPTERIS FILIX–MAS

BUCKLER FERN

HOTTONIA PALUSTRIS

WATER VIOLET

HYDROCHARIS MORSUS–RANAE

FROGBIT

A common fern in temperate regions of the northern hemisphere, this plant is also known in Britain as the male fern. It is a hardy deciduous or semi-evergreen plant, whose mid-green fronds grow from a large crown of dark brown rhizomes to form 'shuttlecocks'. Although the fern is large and sturdy, the fronds arch elegantly, and it is a splendid subject for a bog garden or near a large pond.

Dryopteris dilatata, broad buckler fern, and *D. cristata*, crested buckler fern, also thrive in damp conditions. Buckler fern needs moist soil and shade, but requires little attention other than to cut back dead fronds. Height to 1.2m (4ft); spread 1m (3ft).

This oxygenator floats just beneath the water surface, trailing long white roots that in shallow water will root in the mud of the pond bottom. The submerged, bright green foliage, carried on sturdy stems, is finely divided into feathery leaves. Hottonia is one of the few oxygenators to flower, and in early summer spikes of pale lilac or white flowers – resembling those of primulas, not violets – rise above the water on stems 15–23cm (6–9in) long. Although very hardy, the plant is deciduous and the foliage dies down in late autumn to overwinter as dormant buds.

At first sight, frogbit could be mistaken for a small water lily, but the plant is not rooted and floats freely. It is, however, easily controlled and so is suitable for ponds of all sizes. The fleshy, rounded, greenish bronze leaves, about 2.5cm (1in) across, are produced in rosettes, which both float and stand up above the water. In spring and early summer little white flowers appear, which have three delicate, papery petals and bright yellow centres. Male and female are produced on different plants. *Hydrocharis* is hardy, dying back in autumn and surviving the winter as dormant buds that sprout in spring.

IRIS ENSATA (SYN KAEMPFERI)

JAPANESE FLAG

Most irises do not like to have their rhizomes standing in water, but the attractive Japanese flag is one that does. It is a beardless iris, and instead of the fleshy hairs of the bearded iris has a broad yellow streak on the falls, which tend to be held almost horizontal, rather than drooping. In summer, it bears three or four flowers to a stem; they range from purple to blue, pink, mauve and white and are sometimes bicoloured. The deciduous, narrow, sword-like leaves are deep green, with a pronounced mid-rib. Height: 60–92cm (24–36in).

MENTHA AQUATICA

WATER MINT

A hardy, deciduous marginal plant, ideal for hiding the edges of a pond, water mint is chiefly notable for the aromatic scent that is released when the leaves are crushed. The 2.5–5cm (1–2in) long, hairy, dark green leaves grow on purplish stems that creep along the water's edge. In summer, clusters of small, pale mauve flowers are borne in whorls at the tips of the stems; the flowers are very attractive to bees. This plant is too vigorous for small ponds. Height: 25–45cm (10–18in).

MENYANTHES TRIFOLIATA

BOG BEAN

A scrambling marginal plant that is as happy growing in shallow water as in mud, bog bean is useful for disguising the edge of a pond. Its name derives from the fact that its three-lobed leaves resemble those of the broad bean. They are smooth and rather thick and stand up out of the water, as do the spikes of fringed flowers 1.5cm (½in) across that appear in summer. The flowers are pink in the bud, opening to white. Height: 23–30cm (9–12in); spread 45cm (18in) in 2–3 years.

MYRIOPHYLLUM AQUATICUM
WATER MILFOIL

NUPHAR LUTEA
POND LILY

NYMPHOIDES PELTATA
WATER FRINGE

A mainly submerged oxygenator, water milfoil has whorls of finely divided foliage on stems that can reach 2m (6ft) or more. The beautiful feathery foliage is blue-green, turning reddish in autumn after the first frost where it grows above the water. Insignificant yellowish or pink flowers appear in summer. Fish like to lay their eggs among the stems.

This form is not fully hardy and may need protection in winter, but both *Myriophyllum spicatum* and *M. verticillatum*, which does best in alkaline water, can tolerate a temperature of –20°C (–4°F).

A hardy, native European species, *Nuphar lutea* is useful for giving the effect of a water lily in shade or moving water where water lilies would not thrive. Leathery, heart-shaped leaves up to 38cm (15in) long and 30cm (12in) across float on the surface of the water; beneath the water they are thin and translucent. Round yellow flowers, about 5cm (2in) across, with five sepals and many fine petals surrounding a bottle-shaped fruit, appear in summer. A vigorous plant, suited only to a large pond with water at least 92cm (3ft) deep, it has a strong, rather strange smell. Spread: 2 sq m (6 sq ft) after about 2 years.

This is the only species of *Nymphoides* hardy in cold climates. It resembles a small water lily, with leaves and flowers that float just above the surface from midsummer to early autumn. The mid-green leaves, about 5cm (2in) across, are mottled with brownish purple and are roughly heart shaped, which gives the plant its other common name of floating heart. The large, bright yellow poppy-like flowers have fringed petals like those of the bog bean, to which the plant is related.

In warmer climates, grow *N. humboldtiana*, *N. indica* and *N. aquatica*, all with white flowers.

PERSICARIA AMPHIBIA

AMPHIBIOUS BISTORT

PISTIA STRATIOTES

WATER LETTUCE

PONTADERIA CORDATA

PICKEREL WEED

As its generally used common name implies, this plant is at home both in the water and in soil around the edge of a pond. In a fairly large, deep pool, it does not cause problems, but on land can become invasive. The olive-green, oval leaves give it its other common name, willow grass. The leaves float on the water surface, sending down roots from the nodes of the long stems, and in late summer small spikes of pink or reddish flowers stand up above the water. The plant is deciduous but fully hardy.

Grow bistort in sun or light shade. In water 25–45cm (10–18in) deep, it will put down roots into the pond bottom, but is more easily controlled by planting in a basket, particularly in shallower water.

A floating plant native to tropical and subtropical regions, *Pistia stratiotes* looks like a lettuce with fleshy leaves – hence its name. It is is a member of the arum family and is not hardy, but its rosettes of pale green leaves, some 15cm (6in) across, are so attractive that it is worth growing as an annual in a cold climate. The leaves are fan shaped, strongly ribbed, and have a velvety texture; in summer insignificant white flowers appear among them. Be careful not to splash water on the leaves or they may suffer sun scorch. Water lettuce prefers warm conditions – up to 24°C (75°F) – but will succeed in colder conditions, either in full sun or light shade.

One of the few marginal aquatics with blue flowers, pickerel weed is suitable for ponds of all sizes. Its narrow, heart-shaped, bluish green leaves are smooth and glossy and are held above the water on long stems. The leaves form dense clumps, and all through summer to early autumn flower spikes bearing masses of tiny, soft blue flowers appear among them. Pickerel weed derives its name from the pike that live among it in its native North America.

The variety *Pontaderia lanceolata* has darker blue flowers; in *P. alba* they are white. Pickerel weed needs full sun and is best grown in heavy soil in a planting basket in water 15–30cm (6–12in) deep. Height: 75cm (30in); spread 45cm (18in)

POTAMOGETON CRISPUS

CURLED PONDWEED

PRIMULA VIALLI

ORCHID PRIMULA

RANUNCULUS LINGUA

GREATER SPEARWORT

The strap-like leaves of this completely submerged oxygenator are reminiscent of seaweed. They are dark green to greenish bronze, quite long and tapering, with wavy edges, and have long, wiry stems. In early summer, insignificant reddish brown and white flowers appear just above the water. Although this pondweed does not generally become a nuisance in a larger pond, it spreads fairly rapidly and will need thinning out each year, probably more often in a small pond. The plant is hardy, but deciduous, and dies back to turions, or winter buds.

Potamogeton pectinatus, with grass-like leaves, is also recommended for garden ponds.

Many primulas thrive in the bog garden, but the unusual orchid primula deserves special mention. A hardy perennial with lance-shaped pale green leaves, in midsummer it bears distinctive, densely packed, 7.5–13-cm (3–5-in) long spikes of pale lavender flowers, which are red in the bud. Height up to 30cm (12in).

Other attractive primulas belonging to the Candelabra Group – with their flowers in whorls on the stem – include *P. beesiana*, carmine; *P. bulleyana*, pale orange; *P. helodoxa*, golden yellow. All are 60–92cm (2–3ft) tall.

P. florindae, giant cowslip, with fragrant yellow flowers, reaches 1–1.5m (3–5ft); *P. denticulata*, drumstick primula, has round heads of mauve flowers and grows to only 30cm (12in).

A strong-growing marginal plant, greater spearwort is a tall relation of the buttercup, as its glistening, bright yellow flowers indicate. They are, however, larger – about 5cm (2in) across – and much more showy and are freely produced all through the summer, either singly or in small sprays at the ends of the stems. The blue-green foliage is quite unlike that of the buttercup, the leaves being long and pointed, as the plant's name suggests. It is best grown in a fairly large pond.

Ranunculus flammula, lesser spearwort, lower growing and with smaller flowers, is more suitable for a small pond. Height: 60cm–1.2m (2–4ft).

SCHOENOPLECTUS LACUSTRIS TABERNAEMONTANI 'ALBESCENS'
RUSH

A common evergreen aquatic rush, this plant was previously known as *Scirpus lacustris* and is still often so called. An interesting plant for a bog garden or the margin of a pond, it has sturdy, needle-like, creamy white stems with vertical green stripes, and in summer produces brown spikelets, or tassels of flowers. It grows from creeping stolons and spreads easily, so can become invasive. *Schoenoplectus lacustris tabernaemontani* 'Zebrinus' has round, leafless stems horizontally banded in green and cream. It is also grown in gardens. Height: 96–120cm (3–4ft); spread 60cm (24in) in about 3 years.

STRATIOTES ALOIDES
WATER SOLDIER

A hardy oxygenator, water soldier gets its name from the rosettes of long, pointed, serrated leaves, rather like a pineapple top, which are thought to resemble swords. For most of the year the plant floats just below the water, but in midsummer it rises to the surface, bears small, white, papery three-petalled flowers – male and female on different plants – then sinks and produces large buds. The plant rises again as the buds develop into small plants, which break away from the parent. In winter it sinks to the bottom of the pond, where it lies dormant until spring. Spread: About 1sq m (3sq ft) in a year.

TRAPA NATANS
WATER CHESTNUT

A handsome, unusual-looking plant, water chestnut has rosettes of long-stemmed, diamond-shaped leaves that float on the water surface, buoyed up by spongy leafstalks. The serrated leaves are dark green, sometimes mottled with chocolate. In late summer, in a warm season, small white flowers form in the leaf axils; they are followed by large, edible, black spiny seeds that drop to the bottom of the pond. Often regarded as a perennial, water chestnut is really an annual which cannot tolerate frost and dies back in winter. Grow water chestnut in sun or light shade in still water 30–39cm (12–15in) deep. The seeds lying on the pond bottom will germinate in the mud and produce new plants in the spring.

TYPHA LATIFOLIA

GREAT REEDMACE

This massive, handsome plant is often erroneously called the bulrush. It is a vigorous, hardy marginal, with abundant, rough, grey-green spiky leaves. In mid- to late summer, it produces strong stems with terminal tassels of male flowers that hang above the instantly recognizable, large brown poker-like female flower heads. Although a striking plant, it is far too big and invasive for all but a really large pond in a large garden.

Better species for a smaller pond are the medium-sized *Typha laxmannii*, and *T. minima*, dwarf reedmace, with round brown flower heads, which reaches about 45cm (18in). Height: 1.5–2.4m (5–8ft).

VERONICA BECCABUNGA

BROOKLIME

Grown chiefly for its vivid blue flowers with a white eye, brooklime is an attractive marginal plant. Its trailing stems, clothed in small, round, bright green, fleshy leaves, are ideal for masking the edge of a pool. Dozens of tiny flowers, each only about 8mm ($\frac{1}{3}$in) across, are produced in clusters in the leaf axils all through the summer. With their white eyes, they resemble forget-me-nots, but are generally a deeper blue. The plant is very hardy, and although not fully evergreen it will retain its leaves in a temperature as low as about –20°C (–4°F). Plant brooklime at the pond edge in water up to 10cm (4in) deep; it prefers full sun, but will grow in light shade. Height: 15–20cm (6–8in); spread 45cm (18in) in 2 years.

ZANTEDESCHIA AETHIOPICA

ARUM LILY

Funnel-shaped white spathes and large, glossy leaves make the arum lily one of the most striking plants for pond margins and bog gardens, where it will bloom throughout the summer. The handsome, arrow-shaped leaves, borne on long, smooth stems, are deciduous except in mild areas. Inside the pure white spathe, which can be up to 23cm (9in) long, is a conspicuous golden yellow spadix with tiny flowers, which are sometimes followed by orange seeds.

Slightly smaller but more hardy than the species is *Zantedeschia aethiopica*. 'Crowborough'; 'Green Goddess' has pale green flowers. Height: 45–92cm (18–36in); spread 45–60cm (18–24in).

INDEX

This index lists all the water garden plants, projects and techniques mentioned in this book.
It also comprises entries for essential tools, materials and important ancillary information.
For a general guide to the book, see the list of contents on page 9.

ACKNOWLEDGEMENTS

The majority of the photographs featured in this book have been taken by Neil Sutherland and are © Salamander Books Limited. The publishers wish to thank the following photographers for providing additional photographs, credited here by page number and position on the page, as follows: (B)Bottom; (T)Top; (C)Centre; (BL)Bottom left; etc.

Gillian Beckett: 10, 36(BC), 37(TL), 44(TL), 50(R), 51(TL), 54(L), 55(BR), 58(BR), 59(TR, BR), 61(TR), 63(BR), 124(BL), 128(L, C), 129(L, C), 132(L), 133(L, R), 134(C), 137(C, R)
Pat Brindley: 49(TL), 50(BL)
Eric Crichton 14(BL), 15(TL), 21(TL), 24(B), 25(T), 27(TR), 43(TL), 52(BL), 53(TL, R), 54(B), 55(BL), 57(TC, TR), 58(BL), 59(BL), 62(R), 63(BL), 65(TR), 66(BC), 67(BR), 69(B), 71(T), 74(BL), 76(B), 95(BL), 122 (TL)
Ron & Christine Foord: 60(B)
Garden Picture Library: 41(TR), 65(TL), 113(BC), 132(C)
Garden & Wildlife Matters: 130(L), 131(R)
John Glover: 14(TR), 15(TR, BL, BR), 16(BL), 19(CR), 26, 27(TL), 34(TL), 42(BL), 45(TR), 60(BL), 62(BL), 67(TR), 70(TR), 73(R), 84(L), 110(R), 111(T, BL, BR), 112(TR, BR), 113(BL), 117(T, CR)
Andrew Lawson: 113(BR)
S & O Mathews: 27(B), 65(TC), 75(TL), 76(TL), 77(T, BL), 128(R), 131(L)
Clive Nichols: 13, 18(TR), 23(T), 73(TL), 110(BL), 113(TR)
Maurice Nimmo: 43(TR)
Natural Image/Robin Fletcher: 57(TL), 61(BR) Natural Image/Bob Gibbons: 39(TR), 40, 47(TR), 48(L) 56(L), 63(TL), 130(R), 134(L), 135(L), 136(R)
Derek St Romaine: 113(TL)
Stapeley Water Gardens: 68(C), 69(TL), 70(BL), 71(BR), 72(BL, TR), 74(BL), 75(BR), 77(BR), 129(R), 130(C), 131(C), 132(L), 133(C), 134(R), 135(C, R), 136(L, C), 137(L)

The publishers would like to thank Stapeley Water Gardens, near Nantwich in Cheshire, for providing plants and photographic facilities during the production of this book. Thanks are particularly due to Maria Farmer, Chris Adams, Kim Clarkson, Kevin Walley, Ron Hampson, Barry Sharps and Sarah Davies. The publishers would also like to thank Simon Chapman (Prototype Communications) and Hozelock for supplying pumps and other aquatic equipment for photography. The following companies provided liner and underlay samples for photography: Midland Butyl Liners; Bradshaws; Glass Art Pools; Hozelock.